THE PORTLAND PEERAGE ROMANCE

by Charles J. Archard

originally pulbished 1907

CONTENTS

CHAPTER I

THE FIRST BENTINCK A HERO

What a delightful story is that of the Portland peerage, in which fidelity, heroism, chivalry and romance are blended and interwoven in the annals of the noble families of England. Who that has been to Welbeck Abbey, that magnificent palace in the heart of Sherwood Forest, with its legends of Robin Hood and his merrie men, with its stately oaks and undulating woodlands, stretching away to fertile pastures, dotted over with prosperous farmsteads, as far as the eye can reach, does not feel interested in the fortunes of the noble owner; and who that has seen the Duke and Duchess on some festive occasion at Welbeck, moving to and fro among their thousand guests, a perfectly happy couple, in which the course of true love runs smooth, and whose supreme delight appears to be to spread happiness around them, is so churlish as not to wish them long life, as types of the English nobility it is a delight to honour?

There is no affectation about this illustrious pair, the Duke never poses in relation to affairs of State, and the Duchess has a natural grace all her own, to which art can add no touch of dignity.

Welbeck is now the home of peace and joy; but there have been times when its history has been shrouded in tragic mystery, and even to-day there is the Druce claim to give piquancy to its story.

The family springs from the alliance of the Bentincks and the Cavendishes. Theirs is a telling motto: Dominus providebit (The Lord will provide) was on the crest of the Bentincks, and it befitted a family not too richly endowed with this world's goods according to the position of the Dutch nobility 250 years ago; but being of sterling qualities devoted to the cause they espoused, their descendants have met with their reward. Craignez honte (Fear disgrace) was another motto of the family, and the fear of dishonour has been a characteristic trait from the time when the first Bentinck set foot in England, till to-day.

Before unfolding the drama of tragedy, love, and comedy of these later years let us go back to the tale of heroism surrounding the character of the first Bentinck to make a name for himself in this country. Englishmen are apt to forget the debt of gratitude owing to men of the past; had it not been for Hans William Bentinck this favoured land might still have been under the Stuart tyranny, and the scions of the House of Brunswick might never have occupied the Throne of Great Britain.

James the Second had made an indifferent display of qualities as a ruler, and the nation was tired of a superstitious monarch who was fostering a condition of affairs which was turning England into a hot-bed of religious and political plots and counter-plots. James's daughter, Mary, had married William, Prince of Orange, who was invited to come and take his father-in-law's place as King of England. That invitation was extended in no uncertain way, and James having withdrawn to the continent left the vacancy for his son-in-law and daughter to fill.

When William of Orange came over at the request of many of the nobility and influential commoners in this country there was in his train, Hans William Bentinck, who had previously been to England on a political mission for the Prince.

Bentinck was of noble Batavian descent and served William as a page of honour. His family had its local habitation at Overyssel in the Netherlands and still is known there. At Welbeck a curious old chest, made of metal and carved, is one of his relics, for in it he brought over from Holland all his family plate and jewels.

The Prince was delicate of constitution and his ailments made him passionate and fretful, though to the multitude he preserved a phlegmatic exterior.

To Bentinck he confided his feelings of joy and grief, and the faithful courtier tended him with a devotion which deserves the conspicuous place given to it in English history.

The Prince was in the prime of manhood when he was seized with a severe attack of small-pox. It was a time of anxiety, not only on account of the possible fatal termination of the disease, but in an age of plots, of the advantage that might be taken to bring about his end by means of poison or other foul play.

It was Bentinck alone that fed the Prince and administered his medicine; it was Bentinck who helped him out of bed and laid him down again.

"Whether Bentinck slept or not while I was ill," said William to an English courtier, "I know not. But this I know, that through sixteen days and nights, I never once called for anything but that Bentinck was instantly at my side." Such fidelity was remarkable; he risked his life for the Prince, who was not convalescent before Bentinck himself was attacked and had to totter home to bed. His illness was severe, but happily he recovered and once more took his place by William's side.

"When an heir is born to Bentinck, he will live I hope," said the Prince, "to be as good a fellow as you are; and if I should have a son, our children will love each other, I hope, as we have done."

It was about the time of the Prince's perilous voyage to England to fight, if need be, for the Throne, that he poured out his feelings to his friend. "My sufferings, my disquiet, are dreadful," he said, "I hardly see my way. Never in my life did I so much feel the need of God's guidance."

At this time Bentinck's wife was seriously ill, and both Prince and subject were anxious about her. "God support you," wrote William, "and enable you to bear your part in a work on which, as far as human beings can see, the welfare of His Church depends."

In November, 1688, the Prince landed in England, and with him was Bentinck, accompanied by a band of soldiery, called after his name, as part of the Dutch army. The Prince and his wife were eventually declared King and Queen, and Bentinck experienced substantial proof of the royal favour by being given the office of Groom of the Stole, and First Gentleman of the Bedchamber, with a salary of 5000l. a year. Not long after, in 1689, he was created Earl of Portland, and his other titles in the peerage were Baron Cirencester and Viscount Woodstock; he was also a Knight of the Garter and Privy Councillor. In 1689 he accompanied the King to Ireland and commanded a regiment of Horse Guards, taking part as a Lieutenant-General, in the battle of the Boyne, where his Dutch cavalry did effective service.

He was again at the battle of Namur when William's forces were engaged in fighting the French for the liberties of Europe.

That was in 1695, and in the same year the King once more gave evidence of the affection he bore for his favourite. "He had set his heart," said Macaulay, "on placing the House of Bentinck on a level in wealth and dignity with the Houses of Howard and Seymour, of Russell and Cavendish. Some of the fairest hereditary domains of the Crown had been granted to Portland, not without murmuring on the part both of Whigs and Tories."

It was perfectly natural that William should wish to requite his henchman with rich estates, and in doing so he was acting as other monarchs had done before him, and not upon such good grounds as the services rendered to the State by Bentinck.

Jealousy was, however, aroused among the English nobility at the favouritism shown the Dutch newcomer, and it found strong expression when the King ordered the Lords of the Treasury to issue a warrant endowing Portland with an estate in Denbighshire worth 100,000l., the annual rent reserved to the Crown being only 6s. 8d. There were also royalties connected with this estate which Welshmen were opposed to alienating from the Crown and placing in the hands of a private subject. There was opposition to the grant in the House of Commons and an address was voted, asking the King to revoke it.

Portland behaved with great magnanimity in the matter, his one chief desire appeared to be to avoid a quarrel between his royal friend and Parliament. Not many men would have had such self-abnegation as to renounce an estate estimated to be worth 6,000l. per annum, besides the product of royalties, when they had a King and a victorious army to support them in its possession. The Earl had saved the King's life, he had rendered invaluable services as a diplomatist and General in raising forces to fight for the cause of Protestantism; but for him the probabilities were that James would have retained possession of the Throne and that red ruin would have spread itself over the land. Surely he had won as great a reward as those of the nobility whose only recommendation was that they were the natural sons of royalty.

To have refused this immense estate simply because he was the victim for the time being of racial jealousy is a rare and conspicuous instance in English history of self-sacrifice to honourable motives. His uprightness of character was again tried by the East India Company, who offered him a £50,000 bribe to exert his interest on behalf of that Corporation; but he was not to be tempted by the offer. It will be seen later how the great families, such as Cavendish, became allied with that of Bentinck when the pride of nationality had been reconciled.

Once more in February, 1696, was Portland the means of saving the King's life, through the information he had received of a plot for his assassination by the Papists. The details of the scheme were eventually laid bare and the conspirators brought to justice.

Few men have had a life so full of activity and importance to the State as this Hans William Bentinck. While the Ambassadors were tediously endeavouring at Ryswick to bring about peace between England and France and not making much progress, William took the unceremonious course of sending Portland to have an interview with Marshal Boufflers as representing Lewis. Both were soldiers and men of honour. The meeting took place at Hal, near Brussels, where their attendants were bidden to leave them alone in an orchard. "Here they walked up and down during two hours," says Macaulay, "and in that time did much more business than the plenipotentiaries at Ryswick were able to despatch in as many months."

"It is odd," said Harley, "that while the Ambassadors are making war the Generals should be making peace." In the end the terms these two men negotiated were elaborated in the Treaty of Ryswick, which was the great instrument consolidating William on the Throne, wresting England from the Stuart ascendancy and completing the work of the Revolution.

Such is an outline of the vicissitudes which this extraordinary man passed through in the course of his exciting career. He died in 1709 and was succeeded by his son.

Henry, the second Earl, was Governor of Jamaica, and created Marquis of Titchfield and Duke of Portland in 1716.

His death took place in 1726, and he too was succeeded by his son.

William, second Duke, was a Knight of the Garter, as most of the other holders of the title have been, and he died in 1762. It was through his marriage with the grand-daughter of the Duke of Newcastle that the Bentincks became possessed of Welbeck.

He was succeeded by his son, William Henry Cavendish-Bentinck, third Duke, K.G., who had been M.P. for Weobley. This Duke became Prime Minister of England in 1783, when a Coalition Government was in office. Again in 1807 he was Premier, and was at the head of the Ministry up to shortly before his death in 1809. Other positions held by him were Viceroy of Ireland, Secretary of State for the Home Department, 1794; Lord President of the Council, 1801; Chancellor of Oxford University; High Steward of Bristol and Lord Lieutenant of Notts.; he assumed the additional name of Cavendish by royal licence in 1801. He received his early education at Eton, but in after life declared that he got nothing out of Eton except a sound flogging. It was not claimed for the Duke that he was a man of brilliant attainments, but he was the soul of honour, and for this reputation and for his conciliatory disposition, was chosen to head the Government, which relied for its precarious existence on the reconciliation of the contending parties among the Whigs and Tories. He married the only daughter of the Duke of Devonshire and the male direct line continued in the succession of his eldest son.

The fourth Duke was William Henry Cavendish-Scott-Bentinck, who married Henrietta, eldest daughter of Major-General John Scott, a descendant of Balliol and Bruce, the heroes of Scottish history. There were four sons and six daughters of the marriage, the succession being continued by the second son. The fourth was known as the "Farmer Duke," and with his love of country presuits he lived to the ripe age of eighty-five, dying in 1854.

The most eccentric character in this ducal line was the fifth holder of the title, William John Cavendish-Scott-Bentinck, born in 1800. He was M.P. for Lynn 1824-1826, and died in December, 1879. Of his extraordinary predilections more will be related in succeeding chapters.

The sixth and present Duke is William John Arthur Charles James Cavendish-Bentinck, who was born on December 28th, 1857, and succeeded to the title in 1879. His elevation to the Dukedom is an example of the fortune of birth; the old and eccentric Duke died unmarried, or so it was assumed, and therefore his honours in the peerage passed to his second cousin.

To trace the lineage of the present Duke we must go back to the third Duke, who had a third son (Lord William Charles Augustus). This third son, who was uncle of the eccentric Duke, had issue, Lieut.-General Arthur Charles Cavendish-Bentinck, the father of the present Duke, his mother being Elizabeth Sophia, daughter of Sir St. Vincent Hawkins Whitshed, Bart. The name of Scott was not part of his cognomen; he sprang from another branch in which there was no trace of the Scott element, and the name having been borne by two Dukes for a lady's fortune, there was no further obligation to continue it in connection with the Cavendish-Bentincks.

The marriage of his Grace took place in 1889 to Winifred, only daughter of Thomas Dallas-Yorke, Esq., of Walmsgate, Louth, and their children are: William Arthur Henry, Marquis of Titchfield, born March 16th, 1893, Lady

Victoria Alexandrina Violet, born 1890, and Lord Francis Norwen Dallas, born 1900.

The Duke was formerly a Lieutenant in the Coldstream Guards, then after succeeding to the title, he became Lieut-Colonel of the Honourable Artillery Company of London; he is also Hon. Colonel of the 1st Lanarkshire Volunteer Artillery, and 4th Battalion Sherwood Foresters Derbyshire Regiment. He is Lord Lieutenant of Notts. and Caithness, and was Master of the Horse from 1886-1892 and 1895-1905. He is a family trustee of the British Museum, and is the patron of thirteen livings. The Portland estates comprise 180,000 acres, and his income is estimated at 160,000l. a year from them alone.

Besides Welbeck Abbey, he has country seats at Fullarton House, Troon, Ayrshire; Langwell, Berriedale, Caithness; Bothal Castle, Northumberland, and a London residence at 3, Grovesnor Square.

There are still descendants of the Hon. William Bentinck, eldest son, by the second marriage of the first Earl of Portland. The Hon. William was born in 1704 and created a Count of the Holy Roman Empire in 1732.

The vast fortune of the House of Portland has been built up in a remarkably short space of time, a little over 200 years, and no other great family has received so many honours and acquired such wealth in the same period. In the last century one of the Dukes held fourteen different public offices at the same time, while a younger son was Clerk of the Pipe, and a brother-in-law and nephew had 7,000l. per annum in official salaries; a daughter too was the recipient of a State pension for pin-money.

One of the characteristic traits of the Bentincks has been that in founding the fortunes of the family in the past their scions were successful in capturing great heiresses. These brief genealogical details will help to explain future developments in the history of this noble family.

CHAPTER II

HOW THE BENTINCKS BECAME POSSESSED OF WELBECK,—A FEMININE INTRIGUE

Cherchez la femme is a French saying, which has somewhat of a cynical ring about it. The female hand has to be discovered in the family alliances of the Cavendishes and the Bentincks from which a tangle of intrigue may be unravelled. There was in the first instance that accomplished matchmaker, Bess Hardwick, a country squire's daughter, who was married four times, and from her sprang children and grandchildren with whom were intertwined the families of no less than five Dukes.

To the north of the county of Nottingham, in the heart of England, is a rich and fertile tract of country known as "The Dukeries," once embraced by Sherwood Forest, and even now thickly wooded with magnificent oaks and presenting charming forest scenery.

Its fastnesses were the home of the romantic Robin Hood and his "merrie" band of robbers, the subject of legend and adventure. To-day there are in this beautiful region, within two or three miles of each other, the seats of the Duke of Portland at Welbeck Abbey, the Duke of Newcastle at Clumber, the Earl Manvers (whose family formerly had the title of Duke of Kingston) at Thoresby, and Worksop Manor, formerly the seat of the Duke of Norfolk. It was this cluster of the homes of the nobility that gave it the name of "The Dukeries."

Both Welbeck and Clumber belonged to the Dukes of Newcastle at one time; but to elucidate their settlement upon these vast estates and the subsequent division of the domains, through marriage, we must take up the thread of Bess Hardwick's machinations.

She was the daughter of the Derbyshire squire of Hardwick, and in 1534 was married, when she was only 14 years of age, to Robert Barley, of Barley, in the same county. It was not long before he passed over to the majority, leaving his fascinating widow with a substantial jointure on his property.

For twelve years she was a widow, and then she was married to Sir William Cavendish, who himself had been married twice before.

He was a Hertfordshire magnate, but the strong will of his new wife induced him to sell his estate in that county in order to provide money for another scheme she had in view. It was the ambitious one of purchasing Chatsworth and building the magnificent mansion which tourists from all parts of the world find so much delight in visiting. A house already existed at Chatsworth, but it was not pretentious enough for the squire's daughter, and she prevailed upon her husband to have it demolished. He had started to carry out her wishes when death overtook him, and Bess was a widow for the second time.

The new house at Chatsworth was not finished; but she had a penchant for building, and continued the work after his death till its completion. There were three sons and three daughters of this marriage, concerning the future wedded lives of which there were deep schemes and plots.

Another courtier fell beneath her wiles in Sir William St. Loe, Captain of the Guard to Queen Elizabeth. He was so enamoured of her that he endowed her with his estates, and disinherited his own kinsfolk. Then he died, and Bess still went on conquering and to conquer.

Her fourth husband was the great prize of all, as far as rank was concerned, for he was none other than George Talbot, sixth Earl of Shrewsbury, one of whose seats at that time was Worksop Manor.

It was not Bess's way to accept a suitor without a bargain being made, having ulterior objects. The Earl had been married before, and had children, so that Bess insisted upon two other matrimonial matches before she would enter into the bonds of matrimony herself for the fourth time.

The stipulation was that her daughter, Mary Cavendish, should marry the Earl's heir and his daughter was to marry her son. These alliances were duly entered into, and brought with them new honours and additional wealth. The building of Worksop Manor house had been commenced in the time of the first Earl of Shrewsbury, but was not finished when the new Countess became its mistress. Having built Chatsworth, here was another opportunity for her to display her genius in architecture, and under her direction it was completed, and became a sumptuous residence.

The Earl must have been a nobleman of redoubtable and fearless disposition, or a courtier whose pliant will was easily moulded by accomplished and attractive women, else he would not have been involved in the feminine intrigues that he was.

Not only had he his imperious wife to consider, but he was appointed custodian of Mary Queen of Scots when that unhappy personage was under the ban of Queen

Elizabeth and was sent prisoner to Worksop Manor. She was kept strictly in durance vile, for the Earl was a rigid warder, and did not even allow her to walk in Sherwood Forest.

There is a portrait of Bess of Hardwick in the collection of the Duke of Devonshire at Chatsworth. When Mary was in the custody of her husband Bess first fawned upon her royal prisoner; but a new matrimonial scheme filled her mind which led her to change her conduct into one of hatred. Bess had a grandchild, Lady Arabella Stuart, for whom she planned an alliance hostile to the Queen's interests, hence her smiles were turned to frowns.

En passant it may be said that the Manor went by marriage to the Dukes of Norfolk, who held it for generations and then sold it. Of Bess of Hardwick's building enterprises it may be added that she built Hardwick Hall, "more glass than wall" (according to an old rhyme), in 1587. The Earl died in 1590, and the Countess had another long widowhood of 17 years. Her second son, William Cavendish, was created Baron Cavendish and his great-grandson Duke of Devonshire.

Charles Cavendish was another son of this extraordinary woman, and he bought the Welbeck estate, towards the end of the sixteenth century, from two or three men of obscurity to whom it had passed, after Henry the Eighth had ordered the monastic establishment at the Abbey to be dissolved. His son became Baron Ogle and Viscount Mansfield, and subsequently Earl, Marquis and Duke of Newcastle in 1644.

This nobleman was devoted to the fortunes of Charles I. and was a skilful General during the time of the Civil War.

He also wrote a book on "Horsemanship," which was regarded as a remarkable production of its time, and he built a riding-school at Welbeck, where his theories in the training of horses could be carried into effect; but the structure has in recent years been devoted to other purposes, and a new and more spacious riding-school erected to take its place.

The dukedom became extinct for want of male heirs, but his daughter, Lady Margaret Cavendish, married John Holies, Earl of Clare, who, in 1691, obtained a further step in the peerage by the resuscitation of the dukedom, and once more there was a Duke of Newcastle.

A valuable appointment by the Crown came in his way, for he was chosen Warden of Sherwood, with which office went the privilege of enclosing land at Clumber under the royal prerogative. Again there was no prospect of male heirs, so the Duke left the Clumber property to his sister's son, Thomas Lord Pelham, who traced his descent from Bess of Hardwick through the Pierrepoints (Earls Manvers). Thomas Pelham assumed the name of Holles, and was created Duke of Newcastle-on-Tyne in 1715.

But to return to the Duke who was Warden of Sherwood Forest; he had one daughter, Lady Henrietta Cavendish-Holles, who married Edward Harley, second Earl of Oxford. Their only daughter, Margaret, married William Bentinck, second Duke of Portland.

Hers was a fortunate alliance for the Bentincks. She was a rich heiress, and the vast property at Welbeck and Bolsover belonging to her grandfather, John Holles, was her dowry. This was the first introduction of the Dutch family into Nottinghamshire in 1734.

Having thus traced how this delightful domain passed by matrimonial intrigues into the possession of its present owner, it will be appropriate to glance at the ancient history of the Abbey and see how it has been transformed from its original state to what it now is by successive occupants, and especially by the eccentric fifth Duke.

About the twelfth century a new religious order of monks came to settle in England. They were called Premonstratensians, and wore white cassocks and caps, by which they were known as white canons as distinguishing them from black canons, attired in more sombre garb. About 1140, one Thomas de Cuckney founded the Abbey at Welbeck, which was to become an important centre for the Order, as in 1515 there were no fewer than 35 Premonstratensian monasteries in England, all subordinate in importance to Welbeck.

Thomas de Cuckney was a vir bellicosus, and having built a castle at Cuckney, was a formidable subject during the troublous times of King Stephen's reign. John Hotham, Bishop of Ely, obtained possession of the Manor of Cuckney in the 14th century, and devoted its revenues to the Abbey, with an addition of eight canons to be supported from its wealth.

Then came the edict of Henry VIII., which suppressed monasteries as being detrimental to the State. The abbots and their canons were dispersed, and their lands and property given to royal favourites. Richard Whalley obtained a grant of Welbeck from the King about 1539, and in succeeding generations others who held it were

Osborne, Booth and Catterall, till it was purchased by Sir Charles Cavendish.

This was at the beginning of the reign of James I., and Cavendish inheriting the predilections of his mother, Bess of Hardwick, set to work pulling down the old walls and transforming a house of religion into one for the pleasure of the Dukes that were to come of his family. In 1619, King James paid a visit to Welbeck, and Charles I. was entertained there, when "there was such excess in feasting as had scarcely ever been known in England," and Ben Jonson was present at the invitation of the Duke to enliven the festivities with his wit.

The main portions of the abbey and the abbey church became merged in the new structure; but there are legendary stories that the bodies of the Cuckneys and the abbots remain entombed upon the site, and that their stone coffins form part of massive walls and hidden foundations.

The remains of the ancient Abbey of St. James have been carefully preserved, and the arched ceilings of two or three apartments are interesting examples of the Gothic period. The Servants' Hall is a relic of the monastic buildings, and three other rooms adjacent are in the same style. There is a small doorway with Norman features of architecture, and some roomy vaults and parts of inner walls on which are the effigies of departed monks, indicating the original purpose of the great house as an ecclesiastical establishment.

Bess of Hardwick had a hand in building part of the present mansion, when the domain came into the hands of her third son, Sir Charles Cavendish. Her design, bearing the date 1604, was on the foundations of the old abbey, and still another noble lady added her quota to its architecture. There is the Oxford wing built by the Countess of Oxford, whose daughter Margaret had Welbeck as her dower when she married into the Bentinck family. The Countess had the date 1734 affixed to the wing erected under her auspices. There is the Gothic Hall which was part of her design, and by some is regarded as a gem of its particular style of architecture, with an elegantly-adorned ceiling and fan tracery of stucco on basket-work. The carving is rich and over the fireplace are the Countess of Oxford's armorial bearings.

A tradition exists that Bess acted under the spell of a fortune-teller who predicted that death would be relegated to the distant future so long as she kept on her building operations. It was in 1607 that her end came when her masons could not continue their labours owing to a severe frost, although the urgency of the task was such that they tried to mix their mortar with hot ale. It was a fight with the spectre of death and the spectre won the contest.

She was immensely rich; but could not number a real friend in the world. Chatsworth, Hardwick, Oldcotes, Bolsover and Worksop Manor were either built or partly built under her auspices. Lodge says: "She was a woman of masculine understanding and conduct, proud, furious, selfish, and unfeeling, a builder, a buyer and seller of estates, a money-lender, a farmer, and a merchant of lead and coals."

CHAPTER III

THE FARMER DUKE—WEDS THE RICH MISS SCOTT—HIS HIGH-SPIRITED SONS AND DAUGHTERS

The fourth Duke was known as the "Farmer Duke," from his love of agriculture and rural pursuits, though he was a D.C.L. and F.R.S. and possessed the feudal dignity of Lord Lieutenant of Middlesex. His father had been Prime Minister; but the son made no effort to shine in politics and contented himself with developing the resources of his estates and adding to the wealth of his patrimony.

He had the prescience to choose an heiress for his Duchess and went to Scotland for the purpose.

Major-General John Scott of Balcomie, Fife, had three daughters, the eldest was known as "the rich Miss Scott," the second as "the witty Miss Scott," and the third as "the pretty Miss Scott." The Duke selected Henrietta, "the rich Miss Scott," who besides her wealth had coursing through her veins the blood of Balliol and Bruce, the chieftains of Highland chivalry.

Having secured the hand of the heiress, he assumed by royal licence in 1795, the additional surname of Scott.

Well might the Duke be willing to couple that simple syllable with the patrician accents of Cavendish-Bentinck, for by his marriage with the Fifeshire heiress there came into the family an unexpected windfall of 60,000l. Among the bride's possessions was an island in Scotland, and the Government of the day being desirous of improving the beacon-light, paid 60,000l, for the island and spent about half that sum in addition in erecting a new lighthouse.

Their domestic life was happiness itself, neither was brilliant, but both were honoured by those among whom they lived. The Duchess interested herself in her husband's vast estates, as well as in her own, and in the domestic welfare of their dependants. For a long period she was a fitting companion for the Duke and pre-deceased him ten years, in May, 1844.

Two of their sons developed some remarkable traits and two of the daughters became rich heiresses. The eldest son died young, which opened the way for Lord John to become Marquis of Titchfield and eventually fifth Duke of Portland of eccentric fame. The third was Lord George Bentinck, born on February 27th, 1802. Of the daughters, Lady Charlotte married Mr. Speaker Denison and became Viscountess Ossington and Lady Lucy married Lord Howard de Walden. Clipstone forms part of the Welbeck estate and with the Duke's practical knowledge of agriculture he ordered to be constructed an irrigation system by which he reclaimed thousands of acres of land, formerly rabbit-warrens and swamps, so that they became productive farms. The Duke's flood-dyke, and diversion of the little river Maun for the purposes of drainage, cost him £80,000. His weather-beaten coat and huge leather shoes, extending above the knees, were familiar to the labourers and were characteristic of the simple attire he wore when among them giving instructions as to the laying of his drainpipes.

Many of the oaks on the Welbeck estate were transplanted thither under the fourth Duke's direction, a mechanical appliance being used for the purpose.

One of the lodges in the park was occupied by a porter whose duty was to give beer, wine, bread and cake to any tramping man, woman or child who chose to call.

The Farmer Duke was a lover of horses and racing, though there was nothing mercenary in his connection with the Turf, for he never betted. He took pride in rearing thoroughbred horses at Welbeck and had some of them trained by R. Prince at Newmarket. In the course of his career he had the satisfaction of winning the Derby in 1819 with Tiresias. It was his custom to ride a cob led by a groom, and for the purpose of watching the racing at Newmarket he had a structure placed on wheels which could be moved from point to point, where he could gain a better view of the running through a telescope.

There is an anecdote of the Duke's agility when about eighty years old. He was about to undertake a long walk from Harcourt House; upon which the Ladies Charlotte and Lucy tried to persuade him to ride; but he declined and challenged them to a race. They went into the garden for the purpose and naturally Lady Charlotte won in high spirits.

His death took place at Welbeck on March 27th, 1854, at half-past four in the afternoon, at the age of eighty-five years, having been born in London on June 24th, 1768. His remains were laid to rest in the family vault in the school of St. Mary at Bolsover, the funeral being conducted without pomp, as the executors were limited to an expenditure of £100. The obsequies were not attended by the Marquis, who had not been on friendly terms with his father.

The venerable Duke was immensely rich, for not only had he the patrimony of the Bentincks; but by his marriage with Miss Scott, there was brought into the family another acquisition of wealth.

He left his London property, so that if his son, the Marquis, had no male heirs, it should pass into the female line, which it did, and the first to inherit was the Viscountess Ossington.

This London property was of fabulous value and included Portland-place, Cavendish-square, Wimpole-street, Harley-street, Wigmore-street, and other houses in the neighbourhood.

Lady Ossington died before her sister, so all this wealth came to the Dowager Lady Howard de Walden, furnishing her with the splendid income of 180,000l. per annum.

The stake in the Druce claim is not only the Dukedom of Portland and the entailed estates of the Bentincks in the male line; but in the female line too, including this dazzling dowry of 180,000l. a year.

CHAPTER IV

THE FARMER DUKE'S DAUGHTER AND THE HOUSE OF COMMONS' SPEAKER. — BECOMES A BENEVOLENT VISCOUNTESS

Place aux dames. Before relating some of the incidents in the careers of the fourth Duke's high-spirited sons, the Marquis of Titchfield and Lord George Bentinck, place must be given to the social triumphs of his third daughter, Lady Charlotte Cavendish-Bentinck.

With all the advantages that wealth and birth could give her among the proud aristocracy of England the love affairs of Lady Charlotte did not run smooth. Her lover was Mr. John Evelyn Denison of Ossington Hall, about twenty miles from Welbeck in the same county of Nottingham. That the young Squire — of well-born family though he was — should aspire to the hand of a Duke's daughter showed no want of spirit on his part. But after all he was only a Commoner, though he had in him the making of the First Commoner of England leading to a still higher elevation on the ladder of social distinction, until he became a peer of the realm, only three degrees lower in rank than the head of the Cavendish-Bentincks himself.

The Farmer Duke, simple though his tastes were, did not view with pleasure the courtship of his daughter by the young Squire of Ossington.

Lady Charlotte had mingling in her veins the blood of the highest nobility of three nations. The Cavendishes were among the flower of English chivalry, the Bentincks were renowned in Holland and the Scotts traced their lineage from the pride of Scotland.

The Duke could not bring himself all at once to give Lady Charlotte away to one who had no title.

She was a little over twenty years of age and when her father refused to hear of the suit of John Evelyn Denison she shed many tears in the presence of her maid. Life to her at this time was by no means so full of sunshine as is usually supposed to be the good fortune of Duke's daughters.

At length Lady Charlotte expressed her intention of eloping with Mr. Denison, and at the prospect of indirectly creating a sensation in high life the Farmer Duke relented.

Lady Charlotte's marriage was her first triumph. Her next was when her husband rose to be Speaker of the House of Commons in 1857 and she herself one of the most important personages at the Court of Queen Victoria.

She had become rich and influential, so that when her husband retired from the Speakership he was in a position to tell the Government of the day that he did not intend to take the pension of £5000 a year, to which he was entitled as an ex-Speaker. His refusal was couched in the following words:—"Though without any pretensions to wealth, I have a private fortune which will suffice, and for the few years of life that remain to me I shall be happier in the feeling that I am not a burden to my fellow-countrymen."

Such self-abnegation is not characteristic of many men. On being elevated to the House of Lords he took the title of Viscount Ossington (after the village of Ossington in Notts, which was his ancestral home) and Lady Charlotte was henceforth known as the Viscountess Ossington.

It was a step downward in rank for her, as her marriage with a Commoner did not degrade her to his status. As a Duke's daughter she was still Lady Charlotte and took precedence of Marchionesses, Countesses, and Viscountesses in the etiquette of royal courts and drawing-rooms.

When her husband became a peer she had to take his rank, and it was one of those indefinable sacrifices associated with noble birth, that, as a Viscountess, she had to give precedence to the wives of Marquises and Earls.

To one who had filled so high a position as Lady Ossington had done in political and social life the descent in status involved by the adoption of the new title was not of much moment. She had been honoured by royalty and had done the honours to royalty, she had tasted all the pleasures that aristocratic Society could provide.

Like her brother, the eccentric Duke, Lady Ossington spent large sums of money, intended, directly or indirectly, to benefit the wage-earning classes.

In a spirit of philanthropy she built a coffee palace at Newark, Notts, a town nine miles from Ossington, at a cost of over £20,000. Her object was to provide a hostel where travellers of humble means could find accommodation for the night, at charges within their means, and that it should be a centre of meeting for Friendly Societies and other bodies in their business and social gatherings. The profits of the establishment she directed to be paid to the hospital.

Another coffee palace on similar lines she erected in Marylebone, London, involving an outlay of several thousands.

South African colonization found in her a sympathetic patroness in days when South Africa was little more than a name to the large majority of Englishmen. At her expense in 1886 a party of twenty-four families was sent to the Wolseley settlement, an estate acquired by purchase, about seventeen miles from King William's Town, where full preparations for their reception had been made by a committee. Within two years and a-half the settlement was closed, the cheapness of untaxed drink having changed the settlers from abstainers into drunkards.

The Viscountess was not daunted by this failure to realise her hopes, and in 1888 another attempt at colonization was made under her auspices. Twenty-five families, mostly from Hampshire, sailed for the Cape and formed a new settlement, called by the name of the poet Tennyson. This time the experience of the past was a warning, the enterprise was attended by fairer prospects of success and before her death she had the gratification of knowing that the settlers were contented and happy.

Another of the Duke's daughters was the Dowager Lady Howard de Walden, who became immensely rich on the death of Lady Ossington. Their father had so willed it that if the fifth Duke died without male heirs the London property was to pass to his daughters. Lady Ossington had no children and her rich dowry passed to her sister, who thereby had a double portion. Ossington Hall, after having been for so many years the home of a Duke's daughter, reverted to the Denison family.

From allusions made by Lord George Bentinck to his friends, when he had lost heavily on the turf, it was understood that his mother and sisters, especially Lady

Charlotte, were always ready to help him over his difficulties. It is surmised that they knew more of his secrets and of the secrets of the Marquis of Titchfield than the old Farmer Duke who frowned upon betting transactions and was not known to have been involved in the excitements of a duel and gallantries to actresses, not to mention a nebulous secondary existence as Thomas Druce.

Ossington is within easy carriage distance of Welbeck, but the eccentric brother rarely saw his sister and the latter was astonished at the transformation of the Abbey and grounds brought about by him. Before the alteration of her ancestral home she made an interesting sketch of it, as it was in her father's lifetime.

CHAPTER V

EARLY LIFE OF LORD JOHN BENTINCK, AFTERWARDS FIFTH DUKE OF PORTLAND.— THE ADELAIDE KEMBLE ROMANCE

Lord John Bentinck was born in September 1800, the second son of the fourth Duke. His name in its extended form was William John Cavendish-Scott-Bentinck, and for many years, till the death of his brother Henry, he had no prospect of succeeding to the Dukedom. At nineteen he was a lieutenant in the army, and in 1824 was returned as Member of Parliament for King's Lynn; but the duties of a legislator do not seem to have been much to his taste and he resigned in 1826, his brother, Lord George Bentinck, being elected to take his place.

The fourth Duke kept a large stud of race-horses and Lord John was brought up in the atmosphere of the turf. When a young man he was a horseman, fearless and even reckless in his equestrian exploits. There used to be a gate six feet high at Serlby Hall, the seat of Viscount Galway, which it was said he had jumped one day when hunting.

The three brothers, Henry, John and George, formed a racing partnership under the name of "Mr. Bowes" and were for a time successful in their enterprise, their transactions bringing in considerable sums of money.

The death of the eldest, Henry, in 1824 transformed Lord John into Marquis of Titchfield, heir to the Dukedom and enormous estates of the House of Portland.

With all his splendid advantages of birth and fortune he does not appear to have sought for a wife among the aristocratic families of the land, and it is said that he only made one offer of marriage in his life; at least that was known to his friends. This was to Miss Adelaide Kemble, the celebrated actress.

The tempting proposal was probably made some time between June and October, 1834, when the lady was twenty-five years of age and the Marquis thirty-four.

Judge of his astonishment when she had to confess to him that it was impossible for her to accept his offer as she was already secretly married.

She was at the height of her popularity on the stage, having achieved a splendid triumph in redeeming the fallen fortunes of her family, and though married to another, she cherished kindly remembrances of the noble suitor who made her the proud offer of a ducal coronet.

In reading the "Records" of Fanny Kemble (Adelaide's sister), it is impossible not to be struck with her high ideals and lofty sentiments. Now and then there is an allusion to the Marquis, which shows him in a welcome light and how delicate were his attentions.

On December 1st, 1842, writing to "My dearest Harriet," she says:—"Lord Titchfield, who was here yesterday, begged me to ascertain from you whether it is only my bust that you desire, or whether you would like to have casts from my father's and from the two of Adelaide. Write me word, dear, that the magnificent Marquis may fulfil your wishes, which he is only waiting to know in order to send the one or the four heads to you in Ireland."

Then in a note she explains:—"The Marquis of Titchfield was employing the French sculptor, Dantan, to make busts of my father, my sister, and myself, for him, and most kindly gave me casts of them all, and sent my friend, Miss St. Leger, a cast of mine."

On January 6th, 1843, there is another letter to "Dearest Hal," containing the following allusion:—"I have sent your wishes to Lord Titchfield, and I am sure they will be quickly complied with. I have no idea that he means otherwise than to give you my bust; any other species of transaction being apparently quite out of his line, and giving his especial gift. I have, nevertheless, taken pains to make clear to him your intentions in the matter; I have desired him to have the bust forwarded to the care of Mr. Green, because I thought you would easily find means of transporting it thence to Ardgillan. Was this right?"

"Blessings on Lord Titchfield" invokes Fanny Kemble, in a letter dated from Liverpool, May 4th, 1843:—"I wrote to you last thing last night, dearest Hal, and now farewell! I have received a better account of my father. Dear love to Dorothy, and my last dear love to you. I shall write and send no more loves to anyone. Lord Titchfield—blessings on him!—has sent me a miniature of my father and four different ones of Adelaide, God bless you, dear. Good-bye."

This was not the character of an ogre, and though their marriage could not be, Fanny Kemble evidently thought well of the man, who years afterwards, it was alleged, was leading a double life at this time.

CHAPTER VI

LORD GEORGE BENTINCK'S RACING CAREER. — QUARREL WITH HIS COUSIN. — DUEL WITH SQUIRE OSBALDESTON. — "SURPLICE" WINS THE DERBY AND ST. LEGER. — ATTEMPTS TO POISON THE HORSE. — FRIENDSHIP WITH DISRAELI. — TRAGIC DEATH

One of the great sensations in the middle of the nineteenth century was the mysterious death of Lord George Bentinck, who for many years was the prince of the turf, but who sold his race-horses in order to give more attention to politics and the spread of Protectionist principles, of which he was the leading exponent at that time.

Lord George was born in February 1802, the third son of the Farmer Duke; his elder brother, the Marquis of Titchfield, being that eccentric personage who succeeded to the Dukedom.

After going through the Eton College course and becoming an officer in the Lancers and Life Guards, Lord George took the seat vacated by the Marquis, as M.P. for King's Lynn, in 1826. His life was curiously intermingled with all sorts and conditions of men. Having the hereditary instincts of his family he was a keen votary of the turf and daring early manhood had a partnership with his brother, the Marquis, in the ownership of race-horses, and it was said that at a later time they were both enamoured of Miss Annie May Berkeley, who was the cause of a quarrel between them.

That he was a nobleman of high spirits is evident from the strenuousness with which he lived his short life.

Lord George lost heavily by backing horses for the St. Leger of 1826; the amount was shown to be £30,000, which his mother and sister (Lady Charlotte) helped him to meet. The old Duke, his father, was too cautious to bet, and in order to induce his son to settle down to country pursuits he bought him an estate at Muirkirk, Ayrshire; but the life of a farmer did not suit Lord George for long and he was soon exploiting in horse-racing again, so that in 1833 he was a heavy loser at Goodwood.

He formed studs at Doncaster, Goodwood and Danebury, and at various times his horses were run in the name of Mr. John Bowe, a publican, Mr. King, the Duke of Richmond, and John Day.

Lord George and his cousin, Mr. Charles Greville, were great friends and partners in racing affairs for a time; but both were self-willed and quarrelled, never to heal up their differences.

In the intricacies of their partnership in horses Lord George became the owner of a mare called Preserve, who gained a great reputation about the year 1834.

At the Newmarket meeting there was an attempt to wear down her spirit by false starts, upon which Lord George visited his anger upon his cousin, whom he held responsible.

Years afterwards an attempt was made by Colonel Anson to bring about a reconciliation; but Lord George said he would not have anything to do with "the fellow."

A great stroke was made in 1836 when Lord George won the St. Leger with Elis, it was the first time a horse was conveyed in a van from his training-stable to a race-course.

A specially-constructed vehicle was made and caused consternation among old trainers when they found out the secret of the horse's mode of travelling. Elis was fresh for the race, his advent had been kept a secret, and Lord George won a large sum, one bet being £12,000 to £1,000.

The sensational duel between Lord George and Squire Osbaldeston has passed into the history of racing.

It was 1836, but had its origin in events occurring in 1835. Heaton Park races, near Manchester, attracted a large number of aristocratic jockeys, and Squire Osbaldeston got it into his head that the handicaps were so adjusted as to give the immediate friends of Lord Wilton an advantage.

So the Squire laid himself out to be even with the Wilton party, and when at Doncaster, for the St. Leger, discovered a horse called Rush with powers of running unknown to the sporting clique he desired to circumvent.

The Squire mounted Rush himself and rode him over the St. Leger course, having a mare belonging to Marson the trainer to make the running. Finding that the colt could easily beat, Squire Osbaldeston held him in so that the mare finished the trial a considerable distance in advance.

Rush was consequently given the benefit of the handicapping at Heaton Park and was backed heavily for the cup by the Squire, whose commissioner was ready to meet the Lord Wilton party in any bets they thought well to lay against the colt.

"Two hundred to one against Rush" shouted Lord George Bentinck as Squire Osbaldeston was riding Rush at walking pace past the stand to the starting-post just before the race.

"Done," replied the Squire.

The loud tones of the two men were such as to attract particular notice and the sequel was an exciting one.

The race was brought off and the Squire on Rush won with ease. Then followed a storm of argument as to how and why and wherefore had Rush's powers, so greatly deprecated beforehand, developed to such an extent as to leave all competitors behind.

Another victory was achieved by Rush next day and Squire Osbaldeston having defeated the Wilton clique on the race-course betook himself hunting.

Some months elapsed before the next scene was enacted. Lord George had not settled the bet, and whether he intended to do so or not is an open question. Probably the Squire had not asked him for settlement till the Spring of 1836, when they were brought into contact with each other at the Craven race-meeting.

"My Lord," said the Squire, "May I ask you for the £200 I won from you? You have had time to get over your beating."

"I'm surprised you should ask for the money," replied Lord George, "the affair was robbery; but can you count?"

The Squire rejoined something to the effect that he could count when he was at Eton, and Lord George then counted out a number of banknotes into Osbaldeston's hand.

"It will not end here, Lord George," said the Squire in high dudgeon.

The conversation was at the entrance to the rooms of the Jockey Club, and shortly after it had taken place the Squire sent a second to demand an apology, or that Lord George would fight a duel. The challenge was declined, but the fiery Squire returned to the charge.

"I will pull your nose the next time I see you," was the message he sent to his Lordship, who had no alternative but to meet in a duel or to be subjected to continuous annoyance from the doughty Osbaldeston.

Colonel Anson was named as Lord George's second and the meeting-place was at Wormwood Scrubs at six a.m. The weapons were pistols and the antagonists stood twelve steps apart.

The Squire was a real country sportsman, a fine horseman and a dead shot, his skill with the pistol was such that he could kill pigeons flying and rarely missed, whereas the elegant Lord George was more at home in the boudoir and was unaccustomed to pistol-practice. Osbaldeston had given it out that he would put a bullet through his opponent, which was a rumour not pleasant to reach Lord George's ears.

It was through the finesse of Colonel Anson that the affair ended as it did. By agreement he was to count up to three and when he called the last number both men were to fire.

"One" was uttered with great deliberation.

"Two, three" the Colonel called out in rapid succession, so that the Squire was taken unawares and his shot went an inch or two above Lord George's hair, piercing his hat.

As for Lord George he fired skywards and so the duel ended.

Colonel Anson and Lord George were friends for life, and years afterwards the quarrel with the Squire was so far made up that Lord George invited him to see his horses in training at Danebury. For the greater part of the period between 1830 and 1846 he was regarded as the Dictator of the Turf.

In 1841 he removed his stables from Danebury to Goodwood where his friend, the Duke of Richmond, allowed him every facility on his estate for training horses.

To his honour, be it said, he exercised a powerful influence in endeavouring to rid horse-racing of some of its worst features, and incurred the hostility of the cheats and rogues which have at all times been associated with it.

Finding that a check was being put upon their operations, the welshing fraternity assumed a virtuous attitude and actually put into operation an old statute passed in the reign of Queen Anne, which enabled any private informer to sue and recover treble the amount of a bet made over and above £10. Six writs were served upon Lord George and six upon his partner, Mr. Bowes, in the year 1843, but the plantiff failed to prove the making of the bets and it is obvious that the statute was unworkable. The attempt to put it into force merely shows the condition of racing at the time and the opposition which men who were honourable in their motives had to meet with in their efforts to guard it against reproach, as far as their sporting instincts allowed them.

In 1844 Lord George had as many as thirty-eight horses running in races, and his estimated expenses in 1845 for sixty horses in training were about £40,000, while, the value of the stakes was about £18,000, so that to make racing pay he had to rely upon the success of his betting transactions.

Disraeli called him the "Lord Paramount of the British Turf," which well described his ascendency at the time.

Notwithstanding the magnitude of his bets, Lord George was always cool in temperament while other men who, though they might be quite able to stand a loss, were full of nervous excitement when only a small sum was risked.

He kept on terms of affection with his mother and sisters and he could always rely upon the Duchess for help when his racing extravagances had led him too far.

Lord George was over six feet in stature and his figure was handsome and distinguished. His style of dress was according to the best canons of fashion, elegant and fastidious. A long gold chain was looped upon the breast of his waistcoat and with it he wore costly jewels. He had a new satin scarf of cream colour every day, although the cost of each was about a sovereign.

A frock coat and tall beaver hat completed his costume. His race-course attire consisted of a green coat, top boots and buckskin breeches.

When in Nottinghamshire he used to hunt with the Bufford hounds and kept his hunters at Welbeck.

He was a Freemason, though he does not appear to have had time from his devotion to politics and racing to take any high position in the Order. As to some of his personal habits it may be said that he was not a smoker; but he drank four glasses of wine at dinner-time.

The figure of Lord George has been described by his friend Benjamin Disraeli, afterwards Earl of Beaconsfield, in a few striking sentences thus: "Nature had clothed this vehement spirit with a material form which was in perfect harmony with its noble and commanding character. He was tall and remarkable for his presence; his countenance almost a model of manly beauty; the face oval, the complexion clear and mantling; the forehead lofty and white; the nose aquiline and delicately moulded; the upper lip short. But it was in the dark brown eye that flashed with piercing scrutiny that all the character of the man came forth; a brilliant glance, not soft, but ardent, acute, imperious, incapable of deception or of being deceived."

He was a dandy rivalling d'Orsay, his cravats made other young men of his time envious, and his suits were in the highest style of taste. They were indeed works of art worthy of the genius of Beau Brummell. As for the House of Commons, until he turned serious politician, he treated that old-fashioned assembly with haughty indifference, and when he was pressed to record his vote in party division he entered the House on more than one occasion at a late hour, "clad in a white great-coat, which softened, but did not conceal, the scarlet hunting coat beneath it."

He was a breeder and backer of horses for twenty years, and the recklessness of his wagers staggered the gamblers of his time.

The training of race-horses was brought to a fine art in his day. It had been the custom for owners to send their horses to and fro between Newmarket, Epsom and Doncaster along the high-ways, with the result that although the road hardened their muscles, it militated against their speed.

Lord George raised a protest from some of the old-time patrons of the turf by introducing an innovation in the construction of a large van in which they could travel calmly, without fatigue, these long distances to various parts of England.

It was the precursor of railway travelling then coming into vogue, for Lord George foresaw that the railways would revolutionize racing and enormously increase the votaries of the turf.

After having sat in the House of Commons for 18 years, and taking little interest in the proceedings, Lord George, about 1844, suddenly attracted attention by his attacks on Sir Robert Peel and the Free Traders. He showed an aptitude for Parliamentary business that he had not been credited with in racing circles in which he had held such a leading position. His absorption in politics, which had newly aroused his interest, led him to dispose of his race-horses.

"In the autumn of this year (1846) at Goodwood races," says Disraeli, "the sporting world was astonished by hearing that Lord George Bentinck had parted with his racing stud at an almost nominal price. Lord George was present, as was his custom, at this meeting held in the demesne of one who was among his dearest friends. Lord George was not only present, but apparently absorbed in the sport, and his horses were very successful. The world has hardly done justice to the great sacrifice which he made on this occasion to a high sense of duty. He not only parted with the finest racing stud in England, but he parted with it at a moment when its prospects were never so brilliant; and he knew this well.

"He could scarcely have quitted the turf that day without a pang. He had become the Lord Paramount of that strange world, so difficult to sway, and which requires, for its government, both a stern resolve and a courtly breeding. He had them both; and though the black-leg might quail before the awful scrutiny of his piercing eye, there never was a man so scrupulously polite to his inferiors as Lord George Bentinck. The turf, too, was not merely the scene of the triumphs of his stud and his betting-book. He had purified its practice and had elevated its character, and he was prouder of this achievement than of any other connected with his sporting life. Notwithstanding his mighty stakes, and the keenness with which he backed his opinion, no one perhaps ever cared less for money. His habits were severely simple, and he was the most generous of men. He valued the acquisition of money on the turf, because there it was the test of success. He counted his thousands after a great race, as a victorious general counts his cannon and his prisoners."

Up to the time that he developed a new interest in politics, his great ambition in life had been for one of his horses to win the Derby. And one of the horses that he had owned did win it; but to his chagrin it was no longer his property. That horse was Surplice, the winner in the year 1848; but Lord George had disposed of it with his stud in 1846.

Under any circumstances and whatever the prospects of political success which opened up in Lord George's mind, his decision to dispose of his stud must have caused him a pang as it created a sensation among all who were attracted towards turf doings.

There were two horses in Lord George's stables, which, if he could have laid claim to the powers of divination would have kept him still "Lord Paramount of the Turf." They were the yearlings Surplice and Loadstone, and both were destined to make historic names in the classic races.

But the die was cast and the immense establishment which his friend the Duke of Richmond permitted him to keep on the Goodwood estate was sold.

There were no fewer than 208 thoroughbreds, which all passed into the hands of the Hon. E. M.L. Mostyn, for the small sum of £10,000.

This was in August, 1846, and the light-blue jacket and white cap of Lord George Bentinck were to be seen no more on a race-course.

The stables had been on such an immense scale that the responsibility was too much for one man to undertake, so that the monetary interest was divided, and two or three turf celebrities of the day entered into partnership, which accounts for the fact that when Surplice ran in the Derby of 1848 he was entered in Lord Clifden's name.

From that time to this the career of Surplice has always been of interest to racing men. His trainer was John Kent, who faithfully discharged his duty in guarding the horse from the machinations of unscrupulous loafers and touts.

There was a dead set against the horse. He was naturally a lazy runner and took a great deal of skill to ride. All sorts of rumours were started about him; that he was not well, that he was lame and that he was not the equal of Loadstone, although from the same stable. Up and down went the betting respecting Surplice until the market was in such a state that it was to the interest of an unscrupulous gang to poison or lame him.

Detectives, policemen, trainer and stablemen had to watch him night and day and the excitement waxed intense as the date of the Derby drew near. When the horse was taken from Goodwood to Epsom and from the stable to the course a crowd of horsemen and pedestrians dogged his steps.

Fortunately, with all the precaution taken, Surplice was got into the paddock in fit condition. His jockey was Sim Templeman and after a severe contest Surplice won, there being a neck between him and Springy Jack, while Loadstone was well beaten, to the chagrin of those who had tried to set him off against the better horse Surplice.

The result of the race was £11,000 to the credit of Lord George; but this was nothing compared with his regret that he had not continued the owner of his racing-stud, so that he might have had the honour of winning the Derby in his own name, instead of seeing a horse that he had bred win it in the name of another.

Then came the St. Leger of 1848, and Surplice was again the winner, with further pangs for Lord George. Barely does the same horse win both the Derby and the St. Leger, and proud indeed is the owner who can carry off the blue ribbon of the turf and the St. Leger too. The stars in their courses seemed to be against Lord George at this time.

This is how Disraeli relates the effect the Derby had upon his hero: —

"A few days before, it was the day after the Derby, May 25th, 1848, the writer (Disraeli) met Lord George Bentinck in the Library of the House of Commons. He was standing before the book-shelves with a volume in his hand, and his countenance was greatly disturbed. His resolutions in favour of the colonial interest, after all his labours, had been negatived by the committee on the 22nd, and on the 24th, his horse, Surplice, which he had parted with among the rest of the stud, solely that he might pursue without distraction his labours on behalf of the great interests of the country, had won that paramount and Olympian stake, to gain which had been the object of his life. He had nothing to console him, and nothing to sustain him except his pride. Even that deserted him before a heart which he knew at least could yield him sympathy. He gave a sort of superb groan:

"'All my life I have been trying for this, and for what have I sacrificed it?' he murmured.

"It was in vain to offer solace.'

"'You do not know what the Derby is,' he moaned out.

"'Yes I do, it is the blue ribbon of the turf.'

"'It is the blue ribbon of the turf,' he slowly repeated to himself, and sitting down at the table he buried himself in a folio of statistics."

In a personal allusion to the arduous political labours of Lord George Bentinck, Disraeli says: "What was not his least remarkable trait, is that although he only breakfasted on dry toast, he took no sustenance all this time, dining at White's at half-past two o'clock in the morning. After his severe attack of influenza he broke through this habit a little during the last few months of his life, moved by the advice of his physician and the instance of his friends. The writer of these observations prevailed upon him a little the last year to fall into the easy habit of dining at Bellamy's, which saves much time and permits the transaction of business in conversation with a congenial friend. But he grudged it; he always thought that something would be said or done in his absence, which would not have occurred had he been there; some motion whisked through or some return altered. His principle was that a member should never be absent from his seat."

Disraeli thus describes the last farewell he took of Lord George and his tragic death a few days afterwards:

"He goes to his native county and his father's proud domain, to breathe the air of his boyhood and move amid the parks and meads of his youth. Every breeze will bear health, and the sight of every hallowed haunt will stimulate his pulse. He is scarcely older than Julius Cæsar when he commenced his public career, he looks as high and brave, and he springs from a long-lived race.

"He stood upon the perron of Harcourt House, the last of the great hotels of an age of stately manners, with its wings and courtyard, and carriage portal, and huge outward walls. He put forth his hand to bid farewell, and his last words are characteristic of the man, of his warm feelings, and of his ruling passion: 'God bless you; we must work, and the country will come round us.'"

A few days after this interview Lord George returned to Welbeck.

"Some there were who thought him worn by the exertion of the session, and that an unusual pallor had settled upon that mantling and animated countenance. He himself never felt in better health or was ever in higher spirits, and greatly enjoyed the change of life, and that change in a scene so dear to him.

"On the 21st of September, 1848, after breakfasting with his family, he retired to his dressing-room, where he employed himself with some papers and then wrote three letters, one to Lord Enfield, another to the Duke of Richmond, and the third to the writer of these pages. That letter is now at hand; it is of considerable length, consisting of seven sheets of notepaper, full of interesting details of men and things, and written not only in a cheerful but even in a merry mood. Then, when his letters were sealed, about four o'clock he took his staff and went forth to walk to Thoresby, the seat of Lord Manvers, distant between five and six miles from Welbeck, and where Lord George was to make a visit of two days. In consequence of this his valet drove over to Thoresby at the same time to meet his master. But the master never came. At length the anxious servant returned to Welbeck, and called up the groom who had driven him over to Thoresby, and who was in bed, and enquired whether he had seen anything of Lord George on the way back, as his Lord had never reached Thoresby. The groom got up, and along with the valet and two others, took lanthorns and followed the footpath which they had seen Lord George pursuing as they themselves went to Thoresby.

"About a mile from the Abbey, on the path which they had observed him following, lying close to the gate which separates a water meadow from the deer park, they found the body of Lord George Bentinck. He was lying on his face; his arms were under his body, and in one hand he grasped his walking-stick. His hat was a yard or two before him, having evidently been thrown off in falling. The body was cold and stiff. He had been long dead.

"A woodman and some peasants passing near the spot, about two hundred yards from the gate in question, had observed Lord George, whom at the distance they had mistaken for his brother, the Marquis of Titchfield, leaning against this gate. It was then about half-past four o'clock, or it might be a quarter to five, so he could not have left his home much more than half-an-hour. The woodman and his companions thought 'the gentleman' was reading, as he held his head down. One of them lingered for a minute looking at the gentleman, who then turned round, and might have seen these passers-by, but he made no sign to them.

"Thus it seems that the attack, which was supposed to be a spasm of the heart, was not instantaneous in its effects, but with proper remedies, might have been baffled. Terrible to think of him in his death-struggle without aid and so near a devoted hearth. For that hearth too, what an inpending future!

"The terrible news reached Nottingham on the morning of the 22nd, at half-past nine o'clock, and immediately telegraphed to London, was announced by a second edition of the Times to the country. Consternation and deep grief fell upon all men. One week later, the remains arrived from Welbeck at Harcourt House, to be entombed in the family vault of the Bentincks, that is to be found in a small building in a dingy street, now a chapel of ease, but in old days the Parish Church among the fields of the pretty village of Marylebone.

"The day of the interment was dark and cold, and drizzling. Although the last offices were performed in the most scrupulously private manner, the feelings of the community could not be repressed. From nine till eleven o'clock that day all the British shipping in the docks and the river, from London Bridge to Gravesend, hoisted their flags half-mast high, and minute guns were fired from appointed stations along the Thames. The same mournful ceremony was observed in all the ports of England and Ireland; and not only in these, for the flag was half-mast high on every British ship at Antwerp, at Rotterdam, at Havre.

"Ere the last minute gun sounded all was over. Followed to his tomb by those brothers who, if not consoled, might at this moment be sustained by the remembrance that to him they had ever been brothers, not only in name but in spirit, the vault at length closed on the mortal remains of George Bentinck."

Such was the conventional view which Society took of the sad circumstances of Lord George's death.

The old Duke was over eighty years of age and too infirm to attend the funeral, but the Marquis of Titchfield and Lord Henry Bentinck were present.

As in most mysteries, there were other conjectures more or less improbable.

Years afterwards it was put down to the account of Palmer the poisoner, who it was said had administered strychnine to Lord George as he did to some other members of the aristocracy.

But what was Palmer's motive?

Had Lord George and he any betting transactions together in which Palmer had lost, and finding himself unable to pay, destroyed his noble creditor with diabolical secrecy?

Yet Palmer in 1848 was a young doctor, aged about twenty-three, just setting out on his professional career.

It was not until a few years afterwards that Palmer commenced to turn his attention to turf transactions, therefore it is difficult to find a motive which should be some evidence against him as the perpetrator of this crime.

The case of Palmer was an extraordinary one. He was a medical practitioner at Rugeley in Staffordshire, and having become infatuated with betting had no scruples about removing those to whom he had contracted debts of honour. It was not till the early months of 1856 that light was shed upon some of his fiendish designs and after a long trial he was sentenced to be hanged at Stafford gaol.

Palmer boasted of his racing transactions with the aristocracy, and if Lord George was one of his victims seven years before 1856, the miscreant had had plenty of time to harden his conscience in working his foul plots against others whom it was his sordid interest to destroy.

Another wild theory was that there had been a quarrel between the Marquis of Titchfield and Lord George.

One reason for the dispute was alleged to be that Lord George had been a heavy loser instead of a gainer by his gigantic gambling operations, that he was in want of money, either from his brother the Marquis, or his father, the Duke.

To allege that he was in debt is not consistent with the belief that he had won large sums by backing horses of which he was so keen a judge.

Again it was surmised that the reason for the quarrel—if there was one—was Miss A.M. Berkeley, with whom they were reputed to be both enamoured.

The origin of this lady gives a glimpse of another romance. Her mother was an exceedingly beautiful lady, the daughter of a tradesman, and she became the wife of the Earl of Berkeley.

Fanny Kemble writes of the Countess in terms of admiration; but alludes to the marriage with the addition of the phrase ("by courtesy") and how, on being presented at Court she was frowned at by Queen Charlotte, though George III. did not share the unfavourable sentiments entertained by his wife.

The marriage with the Earl was the subject of a cause celèbre before the House of Lords, with the result that the ceremony was held to be illegal, which thus affected the position of Miss A.M. Berkeley.

Mrs. Margaret Jane Louise Hamilton, a widow lady, the daughter of Mr. Robert Lennox Stuart, made a startling statement which was widely reported in the newspapers at the time that the Druce case assumed a new aspect in 1903. She said that she had been told the details of the death of Lord George Bentinck by her father, who was an eye-witness of the quarrel—if quarrel there was.

Her father was a playmate of the Duke's when they were boys, and she herself was a god-daughter of the fourth Duke.

Not only was Mr. Stuart an eye-witness, but she said Mr. Sergeant, another gentleman, was too.

Lord George was violent in manner towards the Marquis (whom Mrs. Hamilton identified as Mr. Druce) using threatening language towards him and striking him repeatedly.

At last the Marquis retaliated with one blow over the heart, and although it was not a heavy blow, the position where it struck was sufficient to cause death.

Mrs. Hamilton added that she had heard Druce say to her father, "You know, Stuart, I never intended to kill him. I only struck in self-defence."

Druce was remorseful after the tragedy and spoke of surrendering to the police, but Mr. Stuart and Mr. Sergeant persuaded him not to.

Her father said that Druce was nervous and always afraid that the deed would come to light.

Whether the Marquis was there or not to quarrel with his brother, the labourers who said they thought they recognised him, acknowledged that they might have been mistaken.

A point which the evidence at the inquest did not clear up was the whereabouts of the Marquis at the time of the tragedy. The labourers said they thought they saw him.

If it was not he, where was he?

That is a question unanswered to this day.

Lord George was never married, and it has been said of him that "he was notable for the purity of his life."

It was believed that he entertained a deep regard for a highly-placed married lady, whose virtue was beyond suspicion, and hence he lived and died a bachelor.

Three years after the death of Lord George it is said that the Marquis married Miss Annie May Berkeley in the name of Druce.

CHAPTER VII

THE ECCENTRIC DUKE AND HIS UNDERGROUND TUNNELS

The story of the transformation of Welbeck enters upon a new stage with the succession, in 1854, of the Marquis of Titchfield (William John Cavendish-Scott-Bentinck) as fifth Duke, born in 1800. He it was who designed and had constructed the mysterious underground apartments and tunnels for which the Abbey and its environs are famous. There were miles of weird passages beneath the surface of the earth, one tunnel alone being nearly a mile and a half in length, stretching towards Worksop, while others ran in various directions.

Welbeck is nearly 4 miles from Worksop, and a stranger on approaching the Abbey is likely to receive a mean impression of its vast extent. The architecture is a mixture of the Italian and classical styles, and its having been built at different periods, with so many of its adjuncts underground, makes it wanting in imposing features.

In various parts of the estate about 50 lodges were erected for the occupancy of gardeners and keepers. They were of Steetley stone, all similarly planned and pleasing to the eye, what there was of them above ground; but the Duke had subterranean kitchens made at the side and lighted them with bulls'-eyes at the top.

He spent about 100,000l. a year in the development of his plans, and employed as many as 1,500 workpeople in helping him to gratify his hobby. When it is remembered that his reign as Duke lasted a quarter of a century, from 1854 to 1879, it will be seen that artisans of all descriptions found Welbeck a veritable gold-mine. Even so late as November, 1878, a Nottingham newspaper correspondent, on visiting Welbeck, was impressed with its appearance as that of the premises of "some great contractor who had an order for the building of a big village." There was the buzz of machinery, large areas were covered with bricklayers', masons' and joiners' sheds, wherein any new mechanical contrivance was put to the test. For more than eighteen years the vicinity of the house resembled a builder's yard, in the centre of which the Duke lived and moved and had his being, enjoying, in his way, the piles of bricks and mortar surrounding him. After he had decided upon the erection of a new building he had a model of it made for his inspection, and if approved of, it was proceeded with.

Any tramp or wayfarer who applied for work at Welbeck was put on the staff, and the market value of his labour paid. The Duke seemed to find grim pleasure in the society of the casuals who made their way to his stone-yards.

The wing built by the Countess of Oxford in a former generation had a new storey put to it, with a magnificent suite of 14 new rooms furnished in Louis XIV. style, richly gilded, and with mantelpieces of white marble.

An underground passage was made leading to the old riding school, built by the Duke of Newcastle in 1623, but since converted to other uses, such as a library and church, after the erection of the new riding school. Beneath it are great wine cellars with subterranean communications.

The most wonderful of the underground apartments built by the Duke was the picture-gallery, or as it was intended to be, the ball-room. It is lighted from the roof by means of bulls'-eyes. An enormous sum was spent in labour, excavating the solid clay in order that this magnificent saloon might be constructed.

Some choice examples of the great masters are contained in this palace of art, which is 158 feet long, 63 feet wide, and 22 feet high. Here are examples of the works of Sir Joshua Reynolds, de Mytens, Tintoretto, Teniers, Snyders, Bassano, Wyck, de Vos, Greffier, Francks, Berghem, Zucchero, Wootton, Breughel, Dirk Maas, Netscher, Gagnacci, Gerard Honthorst, Van der Meulen, Rigaud, Vandyke, Holbein, Kneller, Lely, Dahl, M. Shee, Knapton, West, Jansen, Verelst; in fact not only in the picture-gallery, but in all parts of the Abbey are scattered treasures of art and vertu. Among the interesting curiosities are the one-pearl drop-earrings seen in the portraits of Charles I., and worn by him on the morning of his execution; also the silver-gilt chalice from which he received the consecrated wine on that fateful morning at Whitehall. The chalice bears the following inscription; "King Charles the First received the communion in this Boule on Tuesday the 30th of January, 1664, being the day in which he was murthered." In the library are autograph letters from the Stuarts, including one from Mary Queen of Scots, signed "Your very good friend."

There is a portrait of Adelaide Kemble, with whom the Duke is said to have been in love in early manhood. The actress is in the pose of her histrionic profession, and in another part of the gallery is a bust of the Duke by H.R. Pinker (1880).

The gigantic riding school is about 380 feet long, 112 feet wide, and 50 feet high, and from it is a subterranean passage leading to the tan gallop, designed for the exercise of horses. The length of this gallop is 1270 feet, and it is all under a glass roof. He had about 100 horses, and his stables extended over an area almost as large as a village.

Of all his extraordinary hobbies that of planning subterranean passages has excited the most wonder and satire. These tunnels, in which it was possible for three persons to walk abreast in some parts, were lighted with gas jets placed at intervals. One at least of the tunnels is large enough for a horse and cart to be driven through.

The drive from Worksop is a delightful one, but all at once the stranger is surprised to find himself in a cavern, leading as might be supposed to the catacombs. It was no uncommon thing for the Duke to rise up out of a tunnel and appear in the midst of a gang of workmen when they were little expecting him, and when, perhaps, they were idling their time, or making uncomplimentary remarks about him.

When the tunnels were in course of construction there might be seen a procession of men on donkeys going to and fro. It was all in a piece with his Grace's conduct that he should purchase donkeys for them to ride upon; but the animals, when let loose, would gnaw at the trees, so the services of the four-legged asses were dispensed with.

His manner of dealing with a strike was a summary one. The wages of the excavators of the tunnels were fifteen shillings a week regularly, sunshine or rain; but the men thought their rich employer could afford them an increase, so they struck.

"You can strike as long as you like," was the message sent by the Duke, "it does not matter to me if the work is never done."

This cool attitude had its effect, the strike was at an end, and the tunnelling proceeded.

One reason given for planning the tunnels was that when he first desired to withdraw himself from observation he tried to close the public rights of way over the estate. This brought him into collision with the powers that be, and he compromised matters to his own satisfaction by making the underground roadways. His cynicism was rich.

"Here have I had provided for you at enormous expense a clean pathway underground, lighted with gas too, and you will persist in walking above ground," was his salute to some astounded visitors. The idea that they should prefer the sunshine, the delightful woodland scenery and sweet-smelling scents wafted over Welbeck in summer-time, to the gaseous tunnels, as if they were rabbits having natural affinities to the burrows of the earth, was one only worthy of a ducal misanthropist.

He was "The Invisible Prince," he liked to take men unawares, he enjoyed a grim joke at their expense, though whether he ever showed signs of merriment, at least in after life, is not so much in the memories of those who knew him, as his eccentricities. He is more associated with the character of an ogre and a cynic who shunned his fellow-men, yet there are some of his employees still living who give him a good word as a kind and considerate master.

There have been various reasons put forth to account for his withdrawal from the society of his peers. It was said that he was smitten with leprosy, that he had an incurable skin desease; then that his love affairs had gone awry when he was a young man, with the result that he became a woman-hater, then a hater of mankind generally.

The Duke was moody and uncertain in his temper. Sometimes he would pass pedestrians in the park without noticing them; at other times strangers would be astonished to hear a shabby old ogre break out at them in profane language because of their intrusion upon his domains, and they would be still more astonished when making complaints about the conduct of this disreputable person, to find that it was the Duke himself.

At that time the use of a traction-engine in agriculture was somewhat of a novelty, and because it was different from the appliances generally used by farmers, was a recommendation to the Duke.

It was nine o'clock one night when he said to his haymakers: "Take the carts home and bring another load with the engine."

"Excuse me, your Grace," said one, "If the engine is made of steel and iron I'm not. I'm tired out."

"Well, perhaps you are, go home then," came the order, which is testimony to the consideration he had for his employees when he was addressed in a manly, straightforward way.

There was a grotesque procession one day at a farm on the Welbeck estate. It was a rainy summer, and the farmers were at their wits'-ends to know how they were to secure their hay in anything like good condition.

The Duke was not a man to be beaten by the weather; he defied it; he was determined to have his grass in the rickyard, wet or dry. So the order went forth that his traction-engine and waggons were to be ready for carrying it on a certain day.

There was to be no shirking, for the Duke's intention was to be with his men to see that the work was done. So he went to the farm in his long brown cape and high silk hat and an umbrella which might have done duty for Hans William Bentinck in the swamps of Holland.

The harvesters filled the waggons in a downpour of rain and the cavalcade started for the homestead. There were three or four waggons behind the engine, and in the last, lo and behold, sat his Grace, grim, silent and self-satisfied that the elements had no terrors for him.

What a life his was to lead; he was a veritable prisoner, having himself for a warder.

The special apartment used by him in the daytime was fitted with a trap-door in the floor, by which he could descend to the regions below, and thus roam about his underground tunnels without the servants knowing whether he was in the house or had left it. By means of this trap-door, after walking to some distant part of his estate and astonishing his workmen there, he could re-appear in the Abbey as mysteriously as he had left it.

The apartment with the trap-door had another door opening into an ante-room, and here his servants received their orders.

The "Prince of Silence" rarely spoke to his attendants; he wrote down on paper what he required and placed it in the letter-box of the door opening into the ante-room. Then he rang a bell, when a servant would come and read what he had written and carry out the order accordingly.

The Duke's bedstead was an immense square erection, constructed in an extraordinary manner. There were large doors to it, so arranged that when folded it was impossible to know whether the bed was occupied by its owner.

He was a lonely traveller, and even when he went to Paris would have no companion with him. His arrangements were made by an avant courier, and when it became known that he had arrived in the gay city, the English aristocracy paid formal visits to him.

These attentions were too much for his habit of loneliness, and he vanished to St. Germains. A few weeks' stay here was enough for him, and he came back to Paris, not lingering more than a couple of days, and then proceeded by stages to Calais and on to London.

One of the best authenticated stories of the fifth Duke relates to his habit of riding alone in a carriage specially constructed to secure privacy. As was natural the more it became known that he wanted to escape observation the more was curiosity aroused to see him, so that a considerable part of his life was spent in adopting stratagems to prevent sight-seers from catching a glimpse of the aristocratic enigma.

The carriage was so made that when the doors were closed no one could see into it, though there were spy-holes arranged that the Duke could look out on all sides and not be observed.

One day the Duke had sent his usual written order for his carriage to proceed by road to London.

The postillions started quite oblivious that they had his Grace with them in his mysteriously-constructed vehicle.

It was a long journey, and as they passed stage after stage, their delays for refreshments became longer and their stoppages more frequent.

They had just pulled up at a country inn when they were horrified to hear a sepulchral voice from the hearse-like chariot shouting,

"What the devil are you stopping for?"

These few words were enough. They came from the voice of the Duke whom they saw not, but recognised by his tones from his tomb on wheels.

The postillions sprang upon the horses and tarried not till they had arrived before the portico of Harcourt House where the great myth descended unseen to his room.

Harcourt House, Cavendish-square, was a famous London mansion, for many years in the possession of the Dukes of Portland. The building of this stately town residence was commenced in 1722 for Earl Harcourt. It had a noble courtyard facing Cavendish-square, and an imposing porte cochère, with a large garden and wide-spreading trees, which were such extraordinary features to be found as adjuncts to the old London palaces of the nobility. Then there was a range of stabling enough to accommodate the stud of a monarch.

This noble mansion was gambled away at a card-party when the stakes were high and the players were the third Duke, grandfather of the eccentric peer, and Earl Harcourt. Thus it came into possession of the Bentincks.

During the occupancy of the fifth Duke, the curious freaks of building for which he was so famous at Welbeck were repeated at Harcourt House. He had the garden enclosed with a gigantic screen of ground-glass, extending for 200 feet on each side and 80 feet high. His object in having this screen constructed was that the residents of Henrietta-street and Wigmore-street might be prevented from seeing into the garden and possibly catching a glimpse of his Grace when taking a stroll.

The gamble for Harcourt House was commuted into a leasehold tenancy by the intervention of the lawyers, who declared that the ownership of the mansion could not be separated from the rest of the estate.

In more recent years the leasehold interest was purchased by the Earl of Breadalbane, and on its expiration, it eventually came to Sir William Harcourt, the statesman, and in August, 1904, was offered for sale. The site of the beautiful garden, with its screen and stables, was purchased by the Post-office authorities. Sic gloria transit of one of the famous houses of London.

Though he had such magnificent palaces, both in Sherwood Forest and in London, the Duke was not given to entertaining guests after the manner of a great noble. His father had sent the family plate to be kept by Messrs. Drummond, bankers, and it was the current belief that the son never had it from the vaults of the bank to grace his tables at Welbeck or Harcourt House.

His sisters seldom visited him, although one of them, Lady Ossington, lived at Ossington Hall, about 15 miles away, in the same county as Welbeck.

The gossips of his lifetime would have it that his pet aversions were tobacco, women, and anyone in the garb of a gentleman; but he had a taste for drinking stout and lived on a simple dietary.

These stories involve a tissue of inconsistencies. His correspondence with Fanny Kemble when he was Marquis of Titchfield, already quoted, shows his kind consideration, not only for her, but for other ladies who moved in higher circles. There was his friendship with Lady Cork, who was often seen by the workmen on the estate driving Shetland ponies. She was a visitor at Cuckney Hall, which was part of the Welbeck domain. Again there are instances on record of his courtesy to those of the opposite sex whom he met in the park; besides which there were many female servants engaged at the Abbey.

"Music hath charms to soothe the savage breast"; but among the other idiosyncrasies laid to his charge, it was said that rather than soothe, it irritated him.

Mrs. Hamilton's testimony is that Mr. Druce (assuming him to have been identical with the Duke) was extremely fond of music, and that she had played to him for hours at a time.

"Sing me the old songs, Stuart" Druce would say to her father, who not only sang, but played the violin.

Moreover the workmen at Welbeck were allowed to have a band which performed at the Abbey on Christmas-eve and the bandsmen were given refreshments.

What a quaint figure the Duke's was. When away from home he wore a wig, but not indoors, his tall hat had a broad brim, he wore a white tie and high collar, his trousers tied round his legs, were of check, with a frock coat and dark waistcoat.

His habits were fastidious, and he would not handle bronze or silver coins before they had been washed. Then he forbade persons to touch their hats to him if they met him.

His manner of dispensing benefactions was characteristic. Sometimes he was lavish in his generosity, while on other occasions he replied in burning words to those who appealed to him.

An instance of the latter is afforded in his reply to the members of a Friendly Society which was in straits for the want of 10l. He told them that if it was a Club established on sound lines, it would be worth their while to subscribe the money among themselves, and if not, he declined to maintain a bankrupt organisation.

He was a devourer of the contents of newspapers, and took all the principal London and provincial daily issues, as well as many weekly journals, which were filed and bound. His bill for one year came to 1,300l. He had four sets of the papers he thought worth preserving, one being at Welbeck, another at Fullarton House, a third at Bothal Castle, and a fourth at Harcourt House. This collection of current literature of the day is believed to be the largest private library outside the British Museum.

In January, 1855, the Crimean War was in progress, and the Duke having given 500l. to the Patriotic Fund, further showed his bounty by ordering that several fat bullocks, 100 head of deer and 1,000 hares should be potted and sent out to the scene of action. Besides these eatables he gave a quantity of unbleached cotton and flannel to be made into shirts and other garments by the ladies of Worksop and district. In that same month Major-General Bentinck, who had been wounded in the right arm, arrived at Welbeck, intending to return to the war as soon as his wound would allow him.

It was formerly the custom for everyone who paid a visit to the stately home in Sherwood Forest, whether on business or pleasure, not to come away without tasting the Worksop ale. Its quality was renowned, and the Duke sent 1,000 gallons of it to the Army fighting in the Crimea.

The lake at Welbeck is three miles long, and its waters are supplied from an irrigation system at Clipstone, costing the fourth Duke 80,000l. to carry out, draining a tract of marshy land and making it one of the most fertile districts in England. After supplying the lake at Welbeck the stream flows to that at Clumber.

It was estimated that between two and three millions sterling were spent by the Duke in putting his ideas into execution, and the one beneficent effect of his expenditure was the employment of a large number of men in work that was not altogether of a useless nature, as witness his great improvements in agriculture, following up his father's ideas, adding to the national wealth by the crops this hitherto uncultivated area was made to produce.

After his long and chequered career the Duke passed away in December, 1879, having nearly reached eighty years of age. Peace be to his ashes.

CHAPTER VIII

THE PRESENT DUKE AND DUCHESS.—A ROMANTIC ATTACHMENT

There must have been a thrilling sensation of delight at the good fortune that had overtaken him when the present Duke found himself in possession of the family honours and estates. There had been so many vicissitudes in the Dukedom that any chance survival might have stepped in to bar his claim. "There's many a slip between the cup and the lip" is an old saying, and many a relation of a great noble is near the succession of his honours, only to see them pass to some other branch where least expected.

The present Duke, or to give him his full family name, William John Arthur Charles James Cavendish-Bentinck, was a long way off the fifth Duke, in the table of consanguinity, he had no trace of the Scott blood in him, and was in fact only second cousin of his eccentric predecessor in the title.

His father was Lieutenant-General A.C. Cavendish-Bentinck, whose descent was through the third Duke, so that the two branches had to go back nearly a hundred years to find a common ancestor. His birth took place on December 28th, 1857, and it must have seemed then a remote possibility that in less than five and twenty years he would succeed to one of the proudest Dukedoms in the land, with the opportunities of a royal alliance.

Two of the Duke's half-brothers were engaged in the South African war; Lord Charles Bentinck was a Lieutenant in the 9th Lancers and was slightly wounded in the siege of Mafeking; for his services he won a medal and a brevet-majority. He was born in 1868 and was educated at Eton; he married in 1897 a daughter of Mr. Charles Seymour Grenfell of Taplow. In the East Midlands he has won considerable popularity as Master of the Blankney Hunt.

Lord William Bentinck was a Captain in the 10th Hussars and showed his ardour in the war by endeavouring to form a body of Colonial Mounted Rifles.

Among the eccentricities laid to the charge of the old Duke it was said that on his young heir going to visit him on one occasion at Welbeck, he ordered him to stand in a corner of the room.

When in 1879 the old Duke passed away from his world of mysteries and escapades, the heir was a Lieutenant in the Coldstream Guards. He was not long in the Army, and when he came into the title there were too many other engagements for him to attend to without troubling himself as to the routine of military duty, though he kept up a connection with the forces by becoming Lieutenant-Colonel of the Honourable Artillery Company of London, Honorary Colonel of the 1st Lanarkshire Volunteer Artillery, and of the 4th Battalion Sherwood Foresters Regiment.

Welbeck soon began to assume a new aspect under his regime. Gradually it lost its appearance of a contractor's yard and looked like one of the stately homes of England.

Looking back to the time when he first came into his noble heritage, the Duke made a touching reference at the Welbeck Tenants' Show, in 1906, to the death of his agent, Mr. F.J. Turner, who for 48 years was in the service of the fifth Duke and himself.

"When I first came to Welbeck, now twenty-seven years ago," said the Duke, "I was a mere boy, very ignorant of the ways of the world, and more ignorant still, if it were possible, of business habits and of the management of a great estate. I shudder to think what might have been my fate, and the sad fate of those dependent upon me, if Mr. Turner and others, who guided my footsteps, had been different from what they proved themselves to be. It was in his power to make or mar the happiness and prosperity, not only of myself, but also of many of those who live in this district and who farm my land."

The Duke followed the traditions of his family and commenced to form an expensive racing stud.

In 1882 his attention was concentrated to a considerable degree upon this object. He bought the famous sire, St. Simon, at the sale of the late Prince Batthyany's horses. St. Simon could not compete in the classic races in consequence of the death of his owner, and all through his racing career he was not put to any severe test of speed, or most likely his name would have represented the double achievement of being a famous racer, and the sire of famous racers too. He was bought for 1,600l., the purchase being effected on the recommendation of Mat Dawson, the trainer, and the horse was then a two-year-old. That he could go at a terrific pace is proved by an observation made one day by Fred Archer to the trainer. St. Simon was at exercise when Archer's spur touched him, unintentionally by the jockey. He bounded into a gallop—a state of action rarely seen before—and Archer subsequently said that he had never been whizzed through the air at such a terrific pace. In the very pink of condition, fresh and strong, the Duke had to congratulate himself on securing his bargain, for he was sent from the course to the stud, with the result that the magnificent total of 246,000l. was won by his progeny in stakes alone.

At length, in 1888, the Duke reached the goal of his ambition in his career on the turf, for he was the winner of the Derby with Ayrshire, which also won the Two Thousand Guineas. Then he followed up his success next year by winning the Derby again with Donovan, a horse that also won the St. Leger.

The names of the mares finding their habitation at Woodhouse Hall, about a mile and a quarter from Welbeck Abbey, are identified with some of the most remarkable successes of the turf. Here is a string of animals through the veins of which ran purest blood. Amoena, Atalanta, Battlewings, Danceaway, Golden Eye, Lady Mar, Larissa, Marquesa, Mowerina, Modwena, Miss Middlewick, Shaker, Semolina, Staffa, Wheel of Fortune, Tact, Ulster Queen, and many besides. The Goddess of Fortune beamed on his Grace's colours whenever they appeared in the great races. The long series of victories resulted in immense winnings. For instance, Modwena was credited with 5,884l.; Ayrshire, 35,915l.; Johnny Morgan, 4,067l.; Donovan, 55,154l.; Semolina, 12,686l.; Miss Butterwick, 8,179l.; Raeburn, 8,374l.; The Prize, 3,134l.; St. Serf, 5,809l.; Memoir, 17,300l.; Schoolbrook, 2,705l.; Amiable, 10,582l.; Other celebrated stock also bred by the Duke included Anna, Charm, Catcher Clatterfeet, Elsie, Eisteddfod, Galston, Katherine II., Little Go, Oyster, Rattleheels, St. Bridget, Simony II., The Task, The Owl, The Smew, Troon, Ulva, and many more. Major Loder's Spearmint was the winner of the Derby in 1906, and it was a bay colt by Carbine—Maid of the Mint, so that a horse owned by the

Duke was again associated with the blue ribbon, Carbine having been imported from Australia by his Grace some years before. Carbine had another name, "Old Jack," given him because of his laziness, and a whip-stock, had to be used occasionally to keep him up to the mark. An Australian picture of the horse was painted by Mr. W. Scott, and after being in the possession of Mr. Herbert Garratt for some years was sent to his Grace with a request that he would accept it, which he did.

All the time that the Duke was paying so much attention to horse-racing it was being asked in Nottinghamshire whether Welbeck was ever to see another Duchess of Portland. The palace of the magician in the heart of Sherwood Forest had not had a mistress for forty years, and the gossips were not diffident in expressing their opinion that it was time the splendour of its hospitality was graced by the presence of a Duchess.

The Duke was thirty-two years of age in 1889, and his name had been coupled with that of a royal princess; but whatever foundation there may have been for the rumour that he was going to marry into the royal family, it was seen eventually that he was determined to wed for love and not for pride of place.

Of the rich and well-born heiresses tracing their lineage through generation after generation of English chivalry, and who would have deemed it the prize of a lifetime to become Duchess of Portland, the Duke's choice fell upon a young lady whose name was unknown to the denizens of Nottinghamshire. She was Winifred, only daughter of Thomas Dallas-Yorke, Esq., of Walmsgate, Louth, and came of an old Lincolnshire family.

She was a merry girl as she used to ride her pony in the Lincolnshire lanes, indeed, she was regarded as somewhat of a tomboy, but a year or two passed away, and she surprised those who had known her in girlhood, to see her the most fashionable beauty in the Row.

She had a wondrous type of beauty too, that made all those who admired its style, fall beneath her spell, her complexion was delicate, yet with the glow of health upon it, her teeth were pearly, her eyes full of sweet reasonableness, her nose that of the classic heroines of Greece, and her willowy form such as Sir Joshua Reynolds would have delighted to paint in a portrait, that would have been one more justification of the poetical phrase, "Art is long and life is fleeting."

Her lithe and graceful figure, nearly six feet in height, with a face pleasing and mobile, and a voice that charmed in its tone, made her distinguished in any society where she appeared.

The story is that once when staying with some friends at Brighton she went to the Devil's Dyke, a romantic place visited by almost every tourist and resident in that neighbourhood. There she was prevailed upon to consult a gipsy as to her future, and the fortune-teller prophesied truth, for the oracular words came forth:—

"You will carry off the greatest matrimonial prize in all England," the gipsy said, as she went through the palmistry study of Miss Dallas-Yorke's shapely hand; "but shortly after your marriage there's trouble of some sort, for the lines become cloudy. I know what it will be, young lady; a terrible illness must attack you, yet take courage and have no fear, my dear, for all will turn out well in the end."

The sequel to the story is that after the happy event of the marriage the gipsy had a black gown and a purse of money presented to her by the Duchess as a compliment to her sagacity as a prophetess.

The latter part of the prediction was fulfilled also, for soon after her marriage the Duchess was attacked by typhoid fever at Welbeck, and her life hung in the balance for a short time during her illness. Happily she recovered to take her place in Society, as graceful and winsome as ever.

She had been out, in the Society sense of the term, several seasons before she became acquainted with the Duke. How the meeting came about is thus related:—

She was on a visit during the autumn of 1888 to a country house In Scotland, and while waiting with her maid on the platform of Carlisle station, she was noticed by the Duke, who was also northward bound for sport on the moors.

The Duke was waiting on the platform too, and was attracted by the perfection of her appearance, her lofty carriage and the expression of the true gentlewoman on her countenance.

A few weeks afterwards an introduction took place at the house of a friend, when they spoke of their recollection of having seen each other on the platform of the railway station.

Although the Duke must have known that he was the most coveted matrimonial prize in England at that time, yet it is said he was shy at proposing to this magnificent daughter of a Lincolnshire squire.

He must have done, however, for in a few months the marriage was celebrated.

Soon after the engagement the Duke bought a sable cloak of immense value for his fiancée; but Mrs. Dallas-Yorke protested against the gift and said that her daughter had not been accustomed to such costly attire.

What was the Duke's observation upon this has not passed current; suffice it to say that the priceless cloak was received and worn by Miss Dallas-Yorke, who in Society was chaperoned by the Marchioness of Granby, now Duchess of Rutland.

Such a fluttering among Society dove-cotes was seldom seen, and sound of wedding-bells rarely heard with such gleeful joy. It was a love-match, and, therefore, a popular event all over the land. Only a few weeks before, the Duke's horse had won the Derby, and the ovation given him by the racing fraternity was unprecedented to any one, peer or commoner, below royal rank.

Then the bride was so full of smiles to all who had the privilege of offering her congratulations.

The Duke had earned the reputation of being a "good fellow," a phrase carrying its own meaning in relation to a typical English nobleman. At the zenith of his popularity there is no wonder that crowds lined the streets on the wedding morning to catch a glimpse of the happy pair as they drove back from Church. The Prince and Princess of Wales honoured the ceremony with their presence, and such cheering there was as the faces of the bride and bridegroom were seen at the windows of the carriage. It was a smart equipage, and even the coachmen and footmen were decorated with horse-shoes of flowers on their coats.

Then there were the rejoicings at Welbeck, where the new Duchess soon ingratiated herself with the tenantry. "The Good Duchess" was smiling and approachable, and quickly found her way to the heart of the most churlish country herdsman.

It was apparent that the Duchess's mind was not solely occupied with plans for reigning in London Society and dictating the fashions for a select and fastidious circle. She knew her powers in that respect; she had already conquered and was content to please the Duke, and fulfil the duties of her station towards those who were her equals, and towards the Duke's retainers on his estates and their dependants.

Not that she ceased to dazzle with the radiant splendour of her jewels, which adorned her natural gracefulness.

Her coronet of diamonds contains in it a lustrous gem, called the Portland stone, worth 10,000l., and her jewels altogether are of fabulous value. Nothwithstanding the changing fashions of High Society, she retains her preference for a Medici collar of lace and a spray of Malmaison carnations.

With the immense sums of money the Duke had won over the Derby victories he was desirous of adding new treasures to his wife's jewel-case; but she prevailed upon him to build some almshouses for poor old women at Welbeck; moreover she is credited with having influenced him to moderate his indulgence in racing.

The almshouses, which were called "The Winnings," have upon them the following inscription: "These houses were erected by the sixth Duke of Portland at the request of his wife, for the benefit of the poor and to commemorate the the the success of his race-horses." They were not built out of money made by betting, a habit not encouraged by the Duke.

At a later period, addressing a meeting of young men, he said: "Turn a cold shoulder to the bookmaker and those who would advise you to throw your money into the lap of fickle Fortune If you want to be happy. You might just as well throw the money into a pond."

The Duchess always has a happy way of opening a Bazaar for some philanthropic object, and her radiant and affable manner charm those with whom she is brought into contact, perhaps for the first time. She is a supporter of the Church Army Training Homes, Bryanston-street, and she has had the courage to preside over a temperance demonstration in Hyde Park. Swimming has become a fashionable accomplishment with Society ladies, and she has shown her interest in extending the cultivation of that exercise. This is only to mention but a few of the objects that claim her time and attention, and no lady of high position is more ready to aid a worthy charity where possible.

The first child that came to the Duke and Duchess was Lady Victoria Alexandrina Violet, born in 1890. She was highly honoured at her christening, for Queen Victoria acted as sponsor person, and held the baby in her arms. There is at Welbeck an autograph letter from the Queen, congratulating the parents on their firstborn. The next was the heir to the Dukedom, William Arthur Henry, Marquis of Titchfield, born March 16th, 1893, and the third Lord Francis Norwen Dallas, born in 1900.

The Duke was Master of the Horse from 1886 to 1892, and from 1895 to 1905; and the Duchess acted as Mistress of the Robes for a short time in 1905, she was also one of the "Canopy Duchesses" at the Coronation.

The Duke's estates in Scotland include Langwell Lodge, which the family has frequently visited for deer-stalking and grouse-shooting in the autumn. Then there is Cessnock Castle, near Galston, Ayrshire, where the Duke and Duchess had not stayed for many years till 1906. A considerable part of the fifth Duke's Ayrshire estates, including the Kilmarnock property, passed at his death to his sister, Lady Ossington, and at her death to another sister, Lady Howard de Walden, and thence to Lord Howard de Walden. The Duke has extensive shootings at Fullarton, near Troon, and Fullarton House was for some time the residence of Louis Philippe of France.

The house of Langwell is situated on a beautiful grassy slope, with the sea in front, while in the background are the silver-clad Scarabines, rising with imposing grandeur. The Langdale and Berriedale rivers here join and flow into the sea, and there are picturesque gorges, with cave-dwellings and ancient ruins having historic associations. Frowning cliffs rise precipitously from the waves, and weird caves, only to be entered when the tide is low, add to the romantic character of the scenery.

In the neighbourhood of this favourite shooting lodge are some steep and dangerous hills which presented great difficulties to the horses when taking his Grace's guests to and fro to enjoy their sport. But having become a votary of the motorcar, these stiff hills have been surmounted with ease by the four or five vehicles which the Duke has acquired for sporting purposes. Helmsdale is the nearest railway station to Langwell, and the road over the Ord of Caithness includes several hills with rough and loose surfaces, and gradients ranging from 1 in 2 to 1 in 16, so that the journey is not without its stress both for horses and motorcars. John o' Groat's is forty-five miles distant, but this, as well as other places of interest in the neighbourhood, is within visiting range by the cars, though such long distances were not attempted with the equine species.

To capture the Master of the Horse as an automobilist was a great achievement for enthusiasts in the advocacy of the new mode of travelling. The Duke of Portland has been such a devotee to the horse, as were his ancestors centuries before him, that it was not to be expected all at once, that he would, give his countenance to any new invention likely to supplant the noble animal in its position as the servant and friend of man. Having been a cyclist, when that hobby seized the fancy of the fashionable world, it was not a long step to automobilism, and having proved the superiority of the motor vehicle, the Duke gave orders for some of the best types of cars to be supplied to him. One of the most luxurious is a Limousine de Deitrich, and his interest in the new art of locomotion is such that he has had a perfect track prepared at Clipstone, called "The flying kilometre."

In 1907 the Duke became a member of the Royal Automobile Club and submitted all his drivers for examination for the certificate. The test took place at

Welbeck, when there were shown several technical drawings executed by the candidates, who all passed with merit and received their certificates.

The Duchess on one occasion made some observations in public on motors, and expressed a doubt as to whether any of her friends would forsake the horse in favour of mechanical locomotion. That time, however, came about, and now the Duchess is claimed as a patroness of the car, which if prosy, compared with the delights of horsemanship, is, nevertheless, useful for accomplishing distances which horses are not expected to cover.

In a speech in the House of Lords, the Duke said he considered the advent of the motorcar could not but have a weakening influence on the horse-breeding industry, and before very long several of the functions which horses at present perform, both in the towns and country districts, would be carried out by mechanical means. His object in making these remarks was to call attention to what was impending in order that some steps might be taken to foster the horse-breeding industry.

As far as a continuance of interest in race-horses is concerned, the Duke had at the commencement of the season 1906 twenty-one horses in training with W. Waugh at Kingsclere, including thirteen two-year-olds.

Both King Edward and the Queen have been entertained at Welbeck since their accession to the throne, and in 1906 there was a visit from the Duke and Duchess of Sparta, the Crown Prince and Princess of Greece.

The Duke's sentiments on "patriotism" may be gathered from some remarks he made when opening a miniature rifle range constructed at the Nottingham High School. He referred with approbation to the work of Mr. Robins, Premier of Manitoba, through whose policy the Union Jack was unfurled from the roof of every school in the province: "The man who objects to perpetuating the glories of the flag, who declines to have his children infused with British patriotism is undesirable." "These words," said the Duke, "apply to the anti-patriot, the pro-Zulu, the pro-Boer, the inciter to rebellion in Egypt, and to the stirrer-up of strife in India. I do not see why rifle-shooting should not become a popular national sport, equal in prestige to games like cricket and football."

CHAPTER IX

THE DUKE AND DUCHESS AT HOME.—THE DUCHESS AS PRINCESS BOUNTIFUL.—THE DUCHESS AT COURT

Christmas is usually spent by the Duke and Duchess at Welbeck, and one of the events of the season is the Household Ball to celebrate the Duke's birthday, which falls on December 28th. It is held in the vast underground picture-gallery, with the subjects of the old painters looking down from their canvases upon the gay dancers.

Choice exotics, stately palms and seasonable shrubs add to the variety of the decorations. The band is almost hidden in a bower of foliage in the centre of the great saloon, and there are 500 guests of all ranks of society from peers and peeresses to the humblest domestic servant.

About ten o'olock the Duke and Duchess appear with their house party, and dancing commences with a Circassion Circle. The Duke has the housekeeper for partner and the Duchess the house-steward, while the aristocratic guests find partners among other chiefs of departments in the Welbeck household.

With midnight comes supper, served in two adjacent underground rooms, that owe their excavation to the grim hobby of the old Duke. All the festive party sit down to supper at the same time, the Duke's French chef providing the menu. The house-steward presides and proposes the health of the ducal family. This is welcomed in the manner it deserves and then dancing is resumed in the picture-gallery.

On another evening the children on the Welbeck estate are invited to a party when the head of a giant Christmas-tree is reared in the centre of the ball-room, laden with toys for distribution to them, and the pleasures of the entertainment are varied with the tricks of a conjurer and ventriloquist. Thus is afforded a glimpse of the happy relations existing between the Portland family and their retainers.

In the neighbourhood of Sutton-in-Ashfield, Cresswell, and the mining district between Mansfield and Worksop the Duchess is regarded as a Princess Bountiful in reality, rather than a creation of fairyland. Her visits to some of the homes of the miners are generally unexpected; for instance one Monday morning in the late autumn she rode up to the unpretending dwelling of a collier to enquire about "an old friend," as she called him, who had worked in Cresswell pits. A few years before he had met with an accident and injured his spine. The occurrence came to the ears of her Grace, who arranged for the patient to visit London to undergo an operation, which he did, with favourable results. A bath-chair was obtained for him and since then she had evinced sympathetic interest in his condition.

As may well be imagined appeals to the Duchess's sympathies are made from all quarters. One day she is taking the chair at the annual meeting of the Children's Hospital at Nottingham. On another day the Nottingham Samaritan Hospital for Women is having her support in the opening of a bazaar in its aid.

Not only suffering humanity, but suffering brute creation has found in her a sympathetic chord. The Bev. H. Russell, who is well known in the county for his efforts on behalf of the Royal Society for the Prevention of Cruelty to Animals, told two interesting stories of her Grace in her presence at the opening of the bazaar.

A show of cab-horses and costermongers' donkeys was being held in Nottingham, when Mr. Russell called the attention of the Duchess to an old rag-and-bone dealer, who had won no prize, but who was known to treat his donkey humanely.

"What shall I give him?" asked the Duchess.

"Half a sovereign will be enough, I should think," replied the clergyman.

She then handed the money to the man, but she had to borrow it though, "and," added Mr. Russell, "I do not know whether she ever paid it back but the result was the same."

When in Scotland once she found that a man with a cart-load of herrings had been using a piece of barbed wire to flog his horse with.

He was taxed with the barbarity, but denied it.

The Duchess thereupon walked back and found the wire. She and the Duke then bought up the horse, cart, harness, and herrings, rejecting the only worthless part of the lot—the man.

Sandy's greed and Sandy's conscience were most likely on a par in their flinty qualities, and the dour Scot would be glad to bargain with the Duchess again on similar terms, eliminating the factor of humanitarianism.

On another occasion she is presiding at the annual meeting of the local branch of the Royal Society for the Prevention of Cruelty to Animals at Grantham. "Such meetings as these," she told her audience, "are valuable because they call attention to the cruelty which exists in such forms as the decrepit horse traffic, of which the general public has little or no knowledge. To be ignorant may save trouble; but if it makes us indifferent and lethargic with regard to suffering, when we ought to be helpers in the cause of humanity, the sooner we increase our knowledge the better we shall be able to stop this great evil and rouse public opinion on the valuable work done by the officers of the Society."

Again she is a visitor at Mansfield to distribute the prizes in connection with singing, needlework, and other competitions organized by the girls' clubs in the district. She spoke of these competitions as promoting a healthy spirit of rivalry, and promised to give a silver shield for proficiency in physical drill among girls.

Her catholic spirit was evinced on her attendance one day early in February, 1907, at the Mikado Café, Nottingham, when the members of a Sunday afternoon Wesleyan Bible Class, numbering ninety men, assembled for dinner. She expressed her interest in the aims of the Bible Class and in all efforts for the encouragement of right living. A bouquet was presented to her from the members.

The Duchess as a flower-seller was a delightful attraction at a Church bazaar at Sutton-in-Ashfield, a town where there is considerable ducal property. In a graceful little speech declaring the bazaar open she said: "I know you are all tired of bazaars and desirous of adopting some better method of collecting money, if such could be devised, but until some brilliant or practical mind finds such a way, you are forced to move in the old groove and repeat the same efforts."

The story of borrowing half a sovereign is not the only well-authenticated instance of her Grace having to negotiate a loan in consequence of her liberal instincts having prompted her to outrun the resources of her pocket.

After opening a bazaar for the Newark Hospital she passed round the stalls and made purchases freely, so that by the time she had made the round she had completely exhausted her purse. It was necessary that she should have enough to pay her railway fare to London, whither she wished to travel, and the honour of tending her the amount she wanted, fell to one of the stewards. The loan, I believe, was promptly repaid.

A Court of exceptional, splendour was held by the King and Queen at Buckingham Palace in May, 1905, and as the then Mistress of the Robes, the Duchess of Buccleugh, was unable to attend through being in mourning, her place was taken by the Duchess of Portland, none eclipsing her in that brilliant throng of English nobility. She wore a gown of ivory velvet, brocaded round the skirt with bouquets of flowers and trimmed with Italian lace and cream chiffon; the train of superb Brussels lace belonged to Marie Antoinette. Her jewels were diamonds, pearls and emeralds.

A brilliant Chapter of the Garter was held in November, 1906, and was followed by a banquet. The regal appearance of the Duchess may be gathered from a description of her dress of cloudy white, embroidered with mother-of-pearl, a high diamond tiara on her dark hair and a magnificent bouquet of flowers, surrounded with a wealth of glittering diamonds on her corsage.

Miss May Cavendish-Bentinck was married to Mr. John Ford on November 3rd, 1906, when Lady Victoria Cavendish-Bentinck made her appearance for the first time as a bridesmaid. Mr. Ford was secretary of the British Legation at Copenhagen and the bride was one of the Duke's cousins. Lady Victoria Cavendish-Bentinck, the Duke's only daughter, will probably be presented at Court next season.

CHAPTER X

CLAIMS TO THE PORTLAND PEERAGE BY MRS. DRUCE AND MR. G.H. DRUCE.

Full of romance as the Portland peerage was up to recent years, there is still another chapter to be added, in relating some of the statements made in connection with the claims put forward by Mrs. Druce and Mr. G.H. Druce to the honours and wealth of the Bentincks. It must be stated emphatically that there is no intention whatever to comment upon these claims or to prejudice their fair consideration, in the tribunals of the land. No literary sketch of the great House of Portland would be complete without it summarised the salient points in the Druce claims as they have appeared from time to time in newspaper reports and in the narratives of those who knew the fifth Duke in his lifetime. This compilation is intended to epitomise the history of the illustrious family of Bentinck in consecutive order of the events as they have occurred, in such a manner as is not found in any other publication; but in no way to influence opinion either on one side or the other. It was in 1898 that public attention was called to the case, when Mrs. Druce set up a claim to the Portland peerage on behalf of her son.

The ground on which it was based was that her father-in-law, Mr. Thomas Charles Druce, and the fifth Duke of Portland were one and the same person; that in fact the Duke had a double existence.

Mr. Druce was in a large way of business at the Baker-street Bazaar, an enterprise opened about 1834 or 1835, with a capital estimated at 100,000l. At that time the Duke had not succeeded to his family estates, but was Marquis of Titchfield. It was known that he and his brothers had been successful in horse-racing and if, as Marquis, he could spare 100,000l. to open this London business, some indication is given of his winnings.

In the construction of the Bazaar it was said that there was an underground passage leading from the back of the premises. By this means of ingress or egress Druce could appear in the midst of his shopmen when they least expected him and as suddenly vanish, possibly into an underground passage, which it was believed was no myth, leading from Baker-street to Harcourt House.

While conducting this important business at Baker-street, Mr. Druce married in 1851 Annie May Berkeley, daughter of the Earl of Berkeley. The Earl's marriage with this lady's mother had been disputed, and was held by the House of Lords to be illegal.

That, however, has no bearing on the Portland romance, the question that arose in 1898 was whether the Duke, under the alias of T.C. Druce, married Miss Berkeley. The strange part of the contention is that Mr. Druce died, or there was a mock burial of his body in Highgate Cemetery, in 1864, whereas the Duke lived on till 1879. The allegation is that there was no death of that particular person in 1864, and that the coffin at the sham funeral was filled with lead or stones.

Mr. Druce had a residence at Holcolmbe House, Hendon, and it was here that he repaired to die.

The funeral was on December 31st, 1864, and the vault was prepared in Highgate Cemetery. There was a stately hearse accompanied by six bearers. The coffin was noticed to be of enormous weight, and the strength of the men were taxed when their duties came to carrying and lowering it into the grave.

From this circumstance arose a curious idea that it did not contain the body of Druce, who was not stout and heavy; but that it was filled with stones or lead. There were no burial certificates forthcoming, but the owners of the cemetery accepted the coffin for burial.

When Mr. Druce died there were two sons left of the alliance with Miss Berkeley, one of whom continued the Baker-street establishment.

But what was the astonishment of some of the frequenters of the purlieus of Baker-street to see the man who was supposed to have been buried visiting the same haunts where they had seen him before.

To have witnessed or heard of the funeral of a man, and then to meet that same man in his customary sphere of business afterwards, is of the nature of a ghost-story. "What did the coffin in Highgate Cemetery contain?" was the riddle.

Mrs. Druce's husband was a son of the late Mr. T.C. Druce, and it was on behalf of her son that proceedings were commenced. She made an application to the Consistory Court for a faculty granting her power to have the coffin in Highgate Cemetery opened in order to see whether it contained a body or only some heavy substance such as lead.

It was asserted that T.C. Druce had been seen alive some years after it was supposed that he had been buried; that he was identified as the Duke of Portland, and that there were persons cognisant of the fact that the Duke and Druce were one and the same person before 1864. Dr. Tristram, the judge, granted the faculty, but notice of appeal was given to prevent the coffin being opened.

The case then came before the Divisional Court, which ruled that the London Cemetery Company was right in resisting the order of Dr. Tristram, and that the grave could not be opened without the licence of the Home Secretary. The decision was in effect that Dr. Tristram had no jurisdiction to make such an order, except as conditional on the authority of the Home Secretary being obtained.

At length the case reached the Court of Appeal in December, 1899, when Mrs. Druce made no appearance to support the faculty she had obtained, and the appeal was dismissed with costs against her.

In the course of the proceedings the statements of two or three persons who knew Mr. Druce were published in the Press.

Mrs. Hamilton's narrative was to the effect that from a girl she had known the same gentleman both as Mr. Druce and the Duke of Portland, her father, Mr. Robert Lennox Stuart, being a great friend of his from boyhood days, and, it was averred, distantly related. There were frequent visits both to Cavendish-square and to the Baker-street Bazaar, and on one occasion, about 1849, Mrs. Hamilton says she was taken by her father to Welbeck where they were met by Druce. Then, in 1851, her father attended the marriage of Druce and Annie May Berkeley. At length the time came when Druce determined to be dead to the outer world. "I must die," he said to Mr. Stuart.

The arrangements for the death were duly carried out and there ensued a sham burial, at which Mrs. Hamilton says her father was present.

Two years passed away and Mrs. Hamilton was greatly astonished one day to see Mr. Druce enter the house where she and her father were staying.

"I thought you were dead," she said naïvely.

Druce was not well pleased at the remark and continued the conversation with her father.

On another occasion Druce took Mrs. Hamilton, then a girl, to Madame Tussaud's, at which her father was angry; he also gave her money for sweets and flowers.

A great many transactions took place between her father and Druce relative to a lady whom they spoke of as "Emmy," and who was eventually sent to France, by Druce, who gave her 5,000l. This was in 1876, and Mr. Stuart went to Welbeck to arrange for the departure with her two children. She died not long afterwards. The last time that Mrs. Hamilton says she saw Druce was in 1876, when he called at her father's and complained of being unwell. He spoke of his visits to his old friend Stuart as being the happiest hours of his life. Some little time after the sham burial Mrs. Annie May Druce came to Mrs. Hamilton's father's house, and was introduced to Mrs. Hamilton as "Mrs. Druce." Another statement was made by Mrs. F. M. Wright, nee Robinson, nee Weatherell, who said that when she was 20 years of age she lived near the Baker-street Bazaar, owned by Mr. T.C. Druce, and frequently saw that gentleman. After the supposed death and burial of Mr. Druce she saw him often, and in her mind he was identical with the Duke of Portland. As to her knowledge of the Duke her father was in the service of his Grace when she was a young girl, and she was familiar with his features. Mr. Druce had a large bump on the left side of his forehead, which appeared to have been caused by a blow. The Duke also had a bump, and in her opinion this resemblance was evidence that the owner of the Baker-street Bazaar and the Duke were one and the same person. While these statements were causing some amount of public interest there was a new development in this extraordinary case. The legal proceedings commenced by Mrs. Druce were widely reported in the Press and accounts of them reached Australia, where they were read by a man pursuing the calling of a miner. His name is Mr. George Hollamby Druce, who put forward a prior claim to the Dukedom than that urged by Mrs. Druce on behalf of her son.

His contention is that the Duke, as T.C. Druce, married in October, 1816, Miss Elizabeth Crickmer, of Bury St. Edmunds, by whom he had a son named George. This youth took to a sea-faring life and eventually settled in Australia, where he had a son, namely Mr. George Hollamby Druce, whose claim to the title takes precedence of that set up by Mrs. Druce for the offspring of the second marriage with Annie May Berkeley.

The question of the exhumation of the body appears to be involved in legal technicalities as to the ownership of the vault. At one time it was vested in the son of Mrs. Druce who commenced the litigation. Then there appeared this other claimant, Mr. George Hollamby Druce, and it is said that the present owner of the vault, Mr. Herbert Druce, is not in favour of complying with Mr. G.H. Druce's wish to open it, therefore the secret of the grave remains unrevealed.

THE END